Central
Highlands

The author and publisher have made every effort to ensure that the information in this publication is accurate, and accept no responsibility whatsoever for any loss, injury or inconvenience experienced by any person or persons whilst using this book.

published by
pocket mountains ltd
6 Church Wynd, Bo'ness EH51 0AN
www.pocketmountains.com

ISBN: 0-9544217-3-6

Copyright © Pocket Mountains Ltd 2004

A catalogue record for this book is available from the British Library

All route maps are based on 1945 Popular Edition Ordnance Survey material and revised from field surveys by Pocket Mountains Ltd, 2002-04. © Pocket Mountains Ltd 2004. Maps on section introduction pages are based on map images © Maps in Minutes™ 2003. © Crown Copyright, Ordnance Survey 2003.

Printed in Poland

Introduction

This guide features forty circular routes in the Central Highlands. It includes all of the Munros (peaks above 914m/3000ft) and many other hills that combine to make good circuits.

Routes have been chosen according to a number of factors, including variety of terrain, great views, historical interest, minimal road walking and the feasibility of a circular route.

Environmental factors such as the ability of access points to support additional cars and opportunities for bypassing visitor-sensitive or eroded areas have also been taken into account. Circular routes help to take the pressure off badly eroded paths, and walking in areas where there have been fewer footsteps is more conducive to natural regeneration of the land.

Walkers can also minimise their own impact on the environment by keeping to purpose-built paths whenever possible and walking in single file to help prevent widening scars. Restricting your use of bikes to tracks, parking sensibly, avoiding fires and litter, and keeping dogs on a lead, particularly on grazing land and during lambing, all help to preserve the land and good relations with its inhabitants. Many of the responsibilities for walkers are now enshrined in law.

How to use this guide

The routes in this book are divided into five regions. These divisions largely represent points of access into the mountains, or use natural geographical boundaries. The opening section for each of the five regions introduces the area, its settlements, topography and key features, and contains brief route outlines. It is supplemented by a road map, locating the walks.

Each route begins with an Introduction identifying the names and heights of significant tops, the relevant Ordnance Survey (OS) map, total distance and average time. Some routes also contain an option for cycling part of the way where there is a long low-level approach.

A sketch map shows the main topographical details of the area and the route. The map is intended only to give the reader an idea of the terrain, and should not be followed for navigation.

Every route has an estimated round-trip time: this is for rough guidance only and should help in planning, especially when daylight hours are limited. In winter or after heavy rain, extra time should also be added for difficulties underfoot.

Risks and how to avoid them

Many of the hills in this guide are remote and craggy, and the weather in Scotland can change suddenly, reducing visibility to several yards. Winter walking brings particular challenges, including limited daylight, white-outs, cornices and avalanches. Every year, walkers and climbers die from falls or hypothermia in the Scottish mountains. Equally, though, overstretched Mountain Rescue teams are often called out to walkers who are simply tired or hungry.

Preparation for a walk should begin well before you set out, and your choice of route should reflect your fitness, the conditions underfoot and the regional weather forecasts.

None of the walks in this guide should be attempted without the relevant OS Map or equivalent at 1:50,000 (or 1:25,000) and a compass.

Even in summer, warm, waterproof clothing is advisable and footwear that is comfortable and supportive with good grips a must. Don't underestimate how much food and water you need and remember to take any medication required, including reserves in case of illness or delay. Many walkers also carry a whistle, first aid kit and survival bag.

It is a good idea to leave a route description with a friend or relative in case a genuine emergency arises: you should not rely on a mobile phone to get you out of difficulty. If walking as part of a group, make sure your companions are aware of any medical conditions, such as diabetes, and how to deal with problems that may occur.

There is a route for most levels of fitness in this guide, but it is important to know your limitations. Even for an experienced walker, colds, aches and pains can turn an easy walk into an ordeal.

These routes assume some knowledge of navigation in the hills with use of map and compass, though these skills are not difficult to learn. Use of Global Positioning System (GPS) devices is becoming more common but, while GPS can help pinpoint your location on the map in zero visibility, it cannot tell you where to go next.

Techniques such as scrambling or climbing on rock are required on only a few mountains in this guide. In winter conditions, take an ice axe and crampons – and know how to use them. Such skills will improve confidence and the ease with which any route can be completed. They will also help you to avoid or escape potentially dangerous areas if you lose your way. The Mountaineering Council of Scotland provides training and information.

For most of these routes, proficiency in walking and navigation is sufficient.

Access

Until the Land Reform (Scotland) Act was introduced early in 2003, the 'right to roam' in Scotland was a result of continued negotiations between government bodies, interest groups and landowners.

In many respects, the Act simply reinforces the strong tradition of public access to the countryside of Scotland for recreational purposes. However, a key difference is that under the Act the right of access depends on whether it is exercised responsibly.

Landowners also have an obligation not to unreasonably prevent or deter those seeking access. The responsibilities of the

public and land managers are set out in
the Scottish Outdoor Access Code.

At certain times of the year there may be
local restrictions, both at low level and on
the hills, and these should be respected.
These often concern farming, shooting and
forest activities: if you are in any doubt, ask.
Signs are usually posted at popular access
points with details: there should be no
expectation of a right of access to all places
at all times.

The right of access does not extend to use
of motor vehicles on private or estate roads.

Seasonal restrictions
Red and Sika deer stalking:
Stags: 1 July to 20 October
Hinds: 21 October to 15 February
Deer may also be culled at other times for
welfare reasons. The seasons for Fallow and
Roe deer (less common) are also longer.
Many estates belong to the Hillphones
network which provides advance notice
of shoots.
Grouse shooting:
12 August to 10 December
Forestry:
Felling: all year
Planting: November to May
Heather burning:
September to April
Lambing:
March to May (Dogs should be kept on
a lead at all times near livestock.)

Glossary
Common Gaelic words found in the text
and maps:

abhainn	river
ailean	field; grassy plain
àirigh	summer hill pasture; shieling
allt	burn; stream
àth	ford
bàn	white
beag	small
bealach	pass; gap; gorge
beinn	ben; mountain
bràighe	neck; upper part
cìoch	breast; hub; pointed rock
clach	boulder; stone
cnoc	hillock
coire	corrie; cauldron; mountain hollow
creachann	exposed rocky summit
creag	cliff
cruach	heap; stack
dubh	black; dark
garbh	thick; coarse; rough
lagan	hollow; dimple
learg	hillside exposed to sea or sun
lochan	small loch; pool
meall	mound; lump; bunch
mór	big; great; tall
sgòrr	peak; cliff; sharp point
sgùrr	large conical hill
stùc	pinnacle; precipice; steep rock

Loch Etive is a vast tidal sea loch. It appears as a crooked arm on the map, extending from the sea in a sweeping curve to force the mountains apart. The upper part of the loch is quiet and little visited but towards bustling Oban it is used commercially for fish farming, with quarrying and forestry on its shores. Caledonian MacBrayne runs ferries from Oban to South Uist, Mull and many of the nearer islands.

This section contains two routes that begin from Victoria Bridge, at the west end of Loch Tulla, a point far from the sea and reached from Bridge of Orchy: the first is a rocky adventure; the second a long traverse over several mountains. An exposed walk on Ben Starav starts at the head of Loch Etive and returns along its shores. Another circuit traverses the length of the Ben Cruachan ridge, returning on the far side of Glen Noe to form a horseshoe. There is also a shorter adventure on a neighbouring peak. The final two walks tackle the rugged peaks at the head of Loch Creran to the north of Oban.

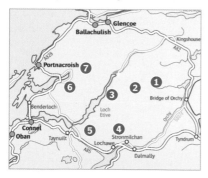

6

Mountains of Loch Etive

The Black Mount

Stob a'Choire Odhair ⓜ(945m),
Stob Ghabhar ⓜ(1090m)

Walk time **7h20** Height gain **1200m**
Distance **18km** OS Map **Landranger 50**

**An exciting circuit of two accessible
peaks with exposure and steep rocky
ground rewarded by views of Rannoch
Moor. This massif has many complex
and steep-sided ridges, making good
navigation essential.**

Start at Victoria Bridge at the west end of
Loch Tulla (GR270423). (Car park south of
the bridge.) Take the waymarked track for

Glen Etive on the north bank of the Abhainn
Shira, and follow it westwards for 1.5km
to the old schoolhouse, a small green
building. Turn right here to follow a good
path north along the east bank of the Allt
Toaig. This passes a great waterfall to the
west as it rises into the amphitheatre.
After 2km, cross a burn and watch for a
smaller path which zigzags steeply up a
prominent rib before fading out. From here,
follow the highest ground to the summit of
Stob a'Choire Odhair (GR257460) (3h).
Descend WSW for 300m to find a good path
which drops westwards to a bealach.

◀ Stob Ghabhar from Rannoch Moor

[Escape: descend into Coire Toaig on the southeast side to join the original path.] From here, it's a short, easy climb westwards until the first rocks begin: the path negotiates the first steep stretch slightly to the north, but then continues directly up scree to the top of the Aonach Eagach ridge. Suddenly, the sides fall away and the spur narrows to a knife's edge, but this soon widens and twists northwest along fenceposts to the summit of Stob Ghabhar (GR230455) (5h). To descend, bear westwards to reach a small knoll after 1km and then descend the south ridge for about

500m in distance until it steepens with crags on both sides. Drop southwest over grassy slopes towards Meall an Araich. Find a grassy track that descends east under the south ridge of Stob Ghabhar before following the Allt Ghabhar down to a plantation. Pass through the trees and cross the burn by the bridge. Follow tracks to reach Clashgour farm. Turn right on the gravel track just before the farmhouse and follow this down to the Abhainn Shira. Take a path downriver (boggy to start) to join a track after 2km, just before the old schoolhouse. Return to the start (7h20).

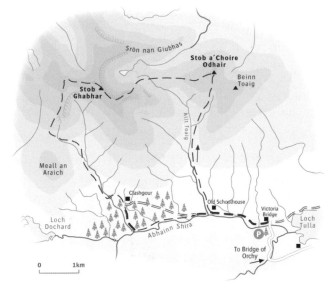

The Scotsman's Corrie

Beinn nan Aighenan ⓜ(960m),
Glas Bheinn Mhór ⓜ(997m),
Stob Coir'an Albannaich ⓜ(1044m),
Meall nan Eun ⓜ(928m)

Walk time **12h + detour 1h40**
Height gain **1700m** Distance **33km**
OS Map **Landranger 50**

An extremely demanding route with a long riverside approach and return. Rough ground, good mountain paths, tricky navigation and fine ridges provide plenty of variety. This route is especially difficult in winter.

Start from Victoria Bridge at the west end of Loch Tulla (GR270423). (Car park south of the bridge.) Take the waymarked track for Glen Etive on the north bank of the Abhainn Shira. Follow the river westwards for 3.5km, first by the track, then on a good path. Cross a bridge over a small burn and continue alongside the main river to a bridge 500m upstream. The grassy track on the south bank is an old cattle route which gains gradual height as it passes Loch Dochard. Drop down over the watershed into upper Glen Kinglass and cross the suspension bridge at Innseag na h-Iuraiche. On the west bank of the river, follow the path south for about 400m. Now leave the path and climb steeply westwards up heather to join the long east ridge of Beinn nan Aighenan. Follow this over 2km of rocky bumps and troughs before the final push to the summit (GR148405) (5h). Descend NNW by a good path which winds steeply to a bealach. Climb the far side to reach a knoll on the main ridge above Glen

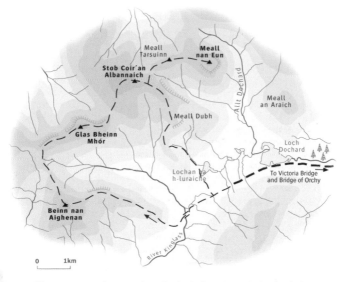

Etive, and bear east to reach a second small knoll. Continue east for a further 1km to gain the top of Glas Bheinn Mhór. This peak has a fine east summit which is easily descended, steepening northeast down to a bealach before the wide scree slopes of Stob Coir'an Albannaich. (Here, an obvious path descends north into Glen Etive.) Climb northeast over steep ground to reach easy-angled grassy slopes above, and continue to the summit plateau of Stob Coir'an Albannaich (GR169443) (8h). Descend east along a fine ridge: this may be corniced in winter. [Detour: about 400m from the summit, drop through broken rock to a

bealach to the north (hard to find). Bear northeast to climb Meall Tarsuinn, drop to another bealach and ascend Meall nan Eun: this peak has steep cliffs on all flanks. Retrace your steps to Stob Coir'an Albannaich (add 1h40)]. Swing southwards on the ridge towards Meall Dubh. From this knoll, it is best to keep to the SSW to avoid steep cliffs on the southeast flank. Descend into Coire nam Ban with its fine burns, and aim for the west end of Lochan na h Iuraiche. Cross the rust-coloured slabs at the head of the lochan and walk south across the bog to join the original path. Follow the Abhainn Shira back to the start (12h).

◀ Loch Tulla and the Etive Hills

Ben Starav from Glen Etive

Ben Starav Ⓜ (1078m)

Walk time **6h40** Height gain **1100m**
Distance **17km** OS Map **Landranger 50**

An entertaining circuit of a classic peak with a high rocky ridge, deep corries and a steep section in descent. This route crosses a variety of terrain, and scrambling skills will be helpful.

Start about 2km from the head of Loch Etive and 1km east of Druimachoish where a track drops down to cross the River Etive by an old bridge (GR137468). (Several parking areas here and westwards.) Immediately after the bridge, turn right to soon gain the cottage of Coileitir. Continue from the house by a path close to the river to reach a footbridge across the Allt Mheuran. Cross the bridge and bear southeast along another path that begins to climb alongside the cascading burn. Two tributaries join after about 600m: do not cross but continue straight on, hugging the west bank of the Allt nam Meirleach as it leads you into a narrowing glen. The slopes here can be boggy after rain but soon lead to firmer, rockier terrain. Climb more steeply into the upper corrie, and keep to the right of a large rock shield to reach a bealach on the main ridge. Climb westwards along the fine craggy spur of Stob Coire Dheirg, an entertaining scramble with steep cliffs and a confusion of pinnacles to the north and a striking quartz seam which bisects the whole mountain. A short exposed section at the top of Stob Coire Dheirg leads to the level summit of Ben Starav. The summit trig point lies a short distance to the northwest (GR125427) (4h). From the top, walk south for about 100m before striking out WSW along a ridge. There is a knoll on the ridge after about 500m, beyond which the ridge descends fairly steeply on a mixture of scree and grass: this is occasionally awkward. Lower down where the spur

becomes less pronounced, head northwest over complex terrain to reach the shores of Loch Etive. Walk northeast along the shore on a good path. Beyond the head of the loch, this passes the private hut at Kinlochetive and leads back to Coileitir and the start (6h40).

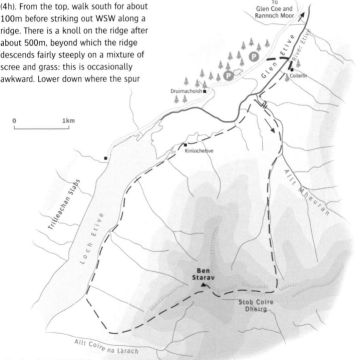

Beinn Eunaich and Glen Strae

Beinn Eunaich ⓜ (989m),
Meall Copagach (810m)

Walk time 5h40 Height gain 1200m
Distance 15km OS Map Landranger 50

One peak, several subsidiary hills and a good ridge make for an interesting journey, with great access and return tracks. This route contains some sections of bog and steep scree, but these are fairly short-lived.

Start at the cottage and greenhouse near the electricity substation, about 2km northwest of Stronmilchan on the B8077 (GR143294). (There are several large parking bays on this road.) Take the track by the cottage which leads north through a gate and towards two farm sheds just beyond. This leads to another track, which branches after 300m. Take the left fork, pass through another gate and begin to climb the gravel track that skirts northwest around the mountain. After gaining good height, the track drops slightly to ford the Allt Lairig Ianachain. Leave the track at about this point and follow the burn upstream. This provides good entertainment with dips and bumps, and waterworn slabs, but can be boggy. Much higher up, you can aim for a large boulder on the skyline close to the bealach between Beinn a'Chochuill and Beinn Eunaich. This gives access to a good path: follow it east as it climbs without difficulty to the summit of Beinn

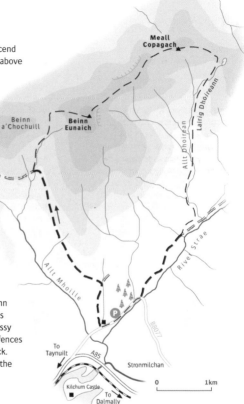

Eunaich (GR135328) (3h). Descend steeply northeast, taking care above the eastern corrie until the terrain eases, to reach a bealach. An undulating climb takes you to a smaller top with its own steep northern corrie and the spoils of landslip. Descend northeast and then continue to the top of Meall Copagach with its complex geology. Drop east: these slopes give a tricky scree descent. Follow the Allt Dhoirean southwards, awkwardly at first where there are small cascades but by an old path lower down. This gives a fast route along the Lairig Dhoireann which contains boggy stretches and is often intersected by grassy farm tracks. The path reaches fences that lead down to a gravel track. Follow this southwest back to the road and the start (5h40).

Big fish of Loch Awe

The great depth and low temperatures of Loch Awe make it an ideal habitat for brown trout. A number of record-breaking ferox brown trout have been caught here, the largest at over 30lb. Local anglers tell of 'yellow bellies' and 'cannibals' but more formal studies of species variation have been undertaken in recent years by the Argyll Fisheries Trust, a charitable body whose remit is to conserve and enhance fish stocks in the area.

◀ Kilchurn Castle on Loch Awe

Ben Cruachan ridge

Ben Cruachan ⓜ (1126m), **Stob Diamh** ⓜ (998m), **Beinn a'Chochuill** ⓜ (980m)

Walk time **10h40** Height gain **2000m**
Distance **25km** OS Map Landranger 50

A strenuous walk with considerable ascent over many rocky peaks makes this a challenging day out. Route-finding skills are essential and scrambling ability will help confidence. This is a particularly hard journey in winter.

Start at the Fisheries, Smokery and Country Park, 2km northwest of Bridge of Awe (GR021317). (Good parking here.) Walk eastwards for 500m towards Bridge of Awe to find a forest track on the left. Follow this northeastwards uphill, taking the left fork after 400m and the right fork shortly after.

Continue for a further 3km through trees and harvested forest to reach the shoreline of Loch Etive. Cross the cattle grid to soon reach a farm. Just before the first farm building, turn right off the track to climb slopes SSE. Pass through a gate, and climb the awkward grassy slopes beyond. After some effort and height gain, these lead to the small rocky outcrops of Meall Copagach where the many peaks of Ben Cruachan come into view. From here on, the landscape is twisted and crumpled, hiding many small pools and steep crags, and making navigation more of a challenge. Bear south over two folding ridges before beginning your ascent of Meall nan Each with its overhanging eastern cliffs. Descend southeast and climb directly up the west face of Ben Cruachan, defended by its kilt of red slabs. Weave your way up, first over scree and then large blocks (sometimes tricky), to gain the west summit of Ben Cruachan. Care is needed on the ridge, particularly in poor visibility,

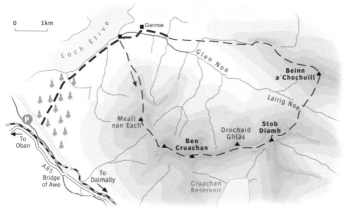

as the northern aspects are uncompromisingly steep and exposed. Descend southeast by a path over scree and boulders before beginning an interesting ascent of the highest top (GR069305) (5h). Descend east for some distance before a further climb towards the top of Drochaid Ghlas. A cairn just before the high point marks a path leading east: follow this steeply at first before it eases off lower down. Continue to the summit of Stob Diamh. Drop northeast and continue to a final top on the ridge. From here, follow the north ridge for about 200m and then take the easiest line northeastwards over grass and boulders to reach the Lairig Noe: this is never difficult but loses much height. [Escape: follow the rough terrain of the glen westwards to Glennoe farm.] From the bealach, tackle Beinn a'Chochuill directly: the steep slopes aid rapid height gain. Higher up, a backbone of granite boulders leads to the summit to give the best panorama of Ben Cruachan (GR109328) (8h). Descend by the gentle west ridge Further down, this splits into two parallel spurs: take the southerly ridge over knolls and folds, losing gradual height into Glen Noe before coming to the end of a track which leads to Glennoe farmhouse. Continue west past the first farm buildings, and back to the start (10h40).

The power of Cruachan

Since 1965, water stored in a reservoir high on Ben Cruachan has been released through turbines into Loch Awe whenever there is a sudden rise in demand for power on the national grid. The televised 1966 World Cup Final at Wembley caused just such a surge and if it hadn't been for the waters of Ben Cruachan, millions of English viewers would not have seen the game into extra-time.

◂ High on Ben Cruachan looking to Loch Etive

Rocky tops of Beinn Sgulaird

Creach Bheinn Ⓒ (810m),
Beinn Sgulaird Ⓜ (937m)

Walk time 6h20 Height gain 1500m
Distance 15km OS Map Landranger 50

A walk to gain the fine ridge of Beinn Sgulaird with views over Loch Creran, Glen Etive and the Isle of Mull. The terrain can be rough going but this route is escapable midway.

Start just north of the house of Druimavuic at a parking bay near the head of Loch Creran (GR008451). A grassy track by a flood warning sign 50m south of the parking bay leads southeast through a forest. After 400m, the track comes to a

gate at the edge of the trees. Beyond the gate, follow a winding gravel track for about 350m to reach an intersection. Take the right fork and pass through another gate after 50m to reach the Allt Buidhe. Cross at a small weir and walk upstream between the deepening ravine and the plantation fence. At the corner of the fence, climb steep heathery slopes southwards to reach the top of the escarpment below Meall nan Caorach. Walk east along the ridge and then south over rough terrain to gain the summit of Creach Bheinn (GR023422) (2h40). From here, follow the undulating ground to the north top. Descend ENE past low castle-like crags and rounded humps to

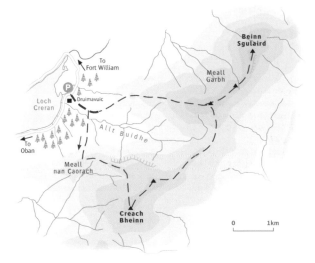

a small bealach. Continue northeast over Creag na Cathaig and down to a bealach and gravel track. [Escape: follow this track west to return directly to the start.] Climb steeply northwards over grass and around crags to a rocky knoll, the most southerly of three tops on the main ridge of Beinn Sgulaird with fine views into upper Glen Etive. Descend northeast, and then climb Meall Garbh, the central top. Lose height again and continue north along the excellent ridge to the summit of Beinn Sgulaird (GR053461) (4h40). Return to the south top. Descend the fine west ridge to reach a wide notch before a rocky knoll and fence: cross the fence by a gate on the right. Climb the knoll, and drop southwest along the ridge by a good path to reach the original track. Retrace your steps back to the start (6h20).

Seal sanctuary

On the shores of Loch Creran, 20km from Oban, the Scottish Sea Life Sanctuary comprises an aquarium and a rescue and rehabilitation facility for common and grey seal pups. Each year a dozen or so pups who have become separated from their mothers are cared for, reared and released back into their natural habitat.

◄ Looking to Buachaille Etive Mór from Beinn Sgulaird

Finlay's Peak

Beinn Fhionnlaidh ⓜ (959m)

Walk time **6h** Height gain **1100m**
Distance **16km** OS Map **Landranger 50**

**A journey into less frequented hills
which offer great views of Glen Etive
and a different perspective on the
Glencoe peaks. Good access tracks lead
to more difficult terrain with few paths.**

Start at a small forestry parking area
marked Elleric, by a fork at the end of the
public road in Glen Creran (GR035488).
Take the right fork past the house of Elleric
and eastwards along the private tarmac
road to reach a collection of farm buildings
at Glenure. Follow the 'public' sign which
directs you left at a junction and then in
front of a long white house to a gateway.
Beyond the gate, turn right immediately to
follow a good track which crosses the river
and continues east along Glen Ure. Keep to
this track for about 1km, passing a large
pond on the left. Before it starts to climb
through the ravine, watch carefully for a
vague grassy track that will lead you
diagonally down to the river and a bridge.
Cross the bridge, and follow the grassy
track to old shielings. At a long wall, leave

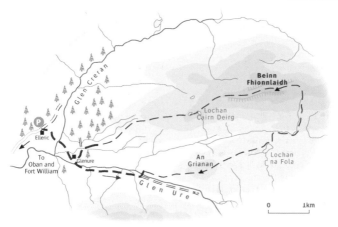

the track and head ESE around boulders and over rough ground to climb the prominent west ridge of An Grianan. This provides an entertaining ascent, with great views over the peaks of Glen Etive from the top GR077478) (2h20). Descend northeast along the increasingly complex and humpy ridge: here it is easier to follow the low ground down to the secluded Lochan na Fola. Climb north over grass to reach a burn after 300m, and then walk upstream through a ravine to reach more level ground. Ascend the long southern slopes of Beinn Fhionnlaidh to reach a bealach to the east of the summit with views of Bidean

nam Bian beyond. A path climbs west, turning rocky buttresses on the left to reach the summit and trig point (GR095497) (4h20). Descend the west ridge where a thin path leads through a mixture of rocks and grass. Where the path fades, drop slightly southwards to reach two lochans. Continue to lose height WSW over more complex ground, passing the occasional perched block. Aim for the southern corner of the large plantation north of Glenure. A gravel track on the fringes of the forest leads through native pine to meet another track. Follow this southwards to reach the farm, and return easily to the start (6h).

Etive by boat

A steamer service from Oban once transported Victorian tourists to the now defunct pier at the north end of Loch Etive, linking with carriages that took them to visit Glencoe. Today, *Anne of Etive* (Loch Etive Cruises) leaves from the pier near Taynuilt during the summer months for 90-minute and three-hour round-trips, an enjoyable way to try to spot seals and golden eagles as well as identifying the magnificent peaks that surround the loch.

◀ Loch Creran in the morning light

The name of Glencoe, synonymous with the unforgiving ruggedness of Scotland in terms of both landscape and history, usually refers not just to Glen Coe itself but to the whole mountain complex between Rannoch Moor and Loch Leven. The River Coe starts close to the inhospitable moor and, after a journey over waterfalls and through the meandering lower reaches, empties into Loch Leven, passing on its

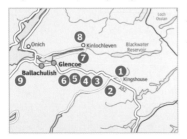

way a trio of steep-sided spurs known affectionately as the Three Sisters: Faith, Hope and Charity.

The view of Buachaille Etive Mór from the east is one of the most celebrated in Scotland: one route tackles this high ridge; another walks along its smaller twin, Buachaille Etive Beag. An adventurous walk in the White Corries begins with a river crossing. The Kingshouse Hotel is the start point for a shorter circuit on Beinn a'Chrùlaiste. An ascent between the Three Sisters provides access to Bidean nam Bian, the highest mountain in this area. Another high and rocky route begins near the National Trust for Scotland Visitor Centre. Loch Leven provides the backdrop for three more routes: the long horseshoe of Beinn a'Bheithir; a route on the Mamores from Kinlochleven; and the Aonach Eagach ridge, described here from the north.

Glencoe and Loch Leven

A Kingshouse round

Beinn a'Chrùlaiste Ⓒ (857m)

Walk time **4h20** Height gain **600m**
Distance **12km** OS Map **Landranger 41**

**Short, uncomplicated route that starts
along the West Highland Way to climb
one peak with views from the top and
an enjoyable descent by a burn.**

Start from the Kingshouse Hotel
(GR259546). Cross the old bridge behind
the hotel and continue along the road to a
junction after 300m. Turn left to follow the
Old Military Road, now part of the West

Highland Way. After about 800m, take the
well-worn path on the right which crosses a
fence by a stile and continues west parallel
to but at some height above the A82. The
path reaches a gate after 3km, close to
some sheep pens and the plantation at
Altnafeadh, to allow the West Highland
Way to access the road. Leave the path at
the gate and start to climb steeply north,
keeping to the right of a fence which slices
up the hillside. Attain the west ridge of
Stob Beinn a'Chrùlaiste and follow this to
its top, a small knoll. Then continue ENE up

◀ Creise and the Kingshouse Hotel

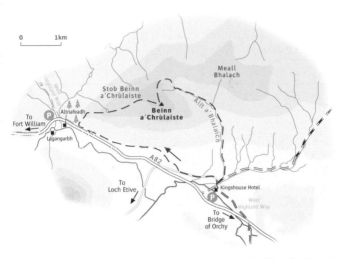

easier folded and often boggy ground to the scree-covered summit of Beinn a'Chrùlaiste (GR246567) (3h). To descend, bear WNW for 400m before taking the northeast ridge which leads to a rounded bealach shared with Meall Bhalach. Descend south and follow the east bank of the Allt a'Bhalaich, which flows in small cascades down to a track: the descent offers unbroken views of Buachaille Etive Mór. Follow this track west to leave you just a few minutes from the Kingshouse (4h20).

Kingshouses

Kingshouses were very basic inns built in the 18th century usually on the sites of construction camps along the 'King's Highways' or military roads in the Highlands. Several are still standing, although only two – Glencoe and Balquhidder – have retained their original name and function. Many fell out of use as inns with the coming of the railway, and others have new names, such as the Inn at Loch Ericht. Glencoe's Kingshouse has been frequented by soldiers, drovers, dam-builders and Charles Dickens through its colourful history and is now a popular stop for footsore walkers on the West Highland Way.

Creise from Glen Etive

Creise ⓜ (1100m), **Meall a'Bhùiridh** ⓜ
(1108m), **Beinn Mhic Chasgaig** (864m)

Walk time 5h20 + detour 1h40
Height gain 1100m
Distance 10km OS Map Explorer 384

A steep climb with optional scrambling, two river crossings (impassable in spate) and tricky navigation in poor weather: a more difficult route in winter. Easy access from the Kingshouse Hotel.

Start from the parking bay by the River Etive, 3km southwest of the A82 (GR227526). Walk northeast along the road for about 800m to the point where two small burns flow under the road to join the River Etive. Here, large slabs of rock make this an easy crossing in good conditions (this would be inadvisable when the river is in spate, and better to walk in from the

A82). From the other bank, cross steepening grass slopes in a southeasterly direction towards the pronounced north ridge of Sròn na Creise. Weave through the few broken buttresses to reach the first main tower. This can be easily traversed by climbing scree on the right hand side. The next obstacle is a long buttress which rises from left to right. Again, this can be easily negotiated on the right to the top of the scree chute. [Variant: climb this buttress, starting at the lower left end where there is a visible notch. Scramble up exposed slabs and continue with interest up the ridge to reach the top of the chute.] The next section can be traversed on the left by a grassy path which leads to easy ground. [Variant: climb directly up the apex, with some hard moves to start.] Easier terrain is followed to the top of Stob a'Ghlais Choire,

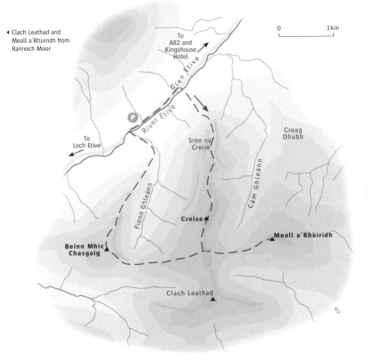

◀ Clach Leathad and Meall a'Bhùiridh from Rannoch Moor

To A82 and Kingshouse Hotel

Glen Etive

River Etive

P

To Loch Etive

Sròn na Creise

Creag Dhubh

Cam Ghleann

Fionn Ghleann

Creise ▲

Meall a'Bhùiridh

Beinn Mhic Chasgaig ▲

Clach Leathad ▲

0   1km

a rocky knoll with cliffs to the east. Continue southwards around the corrie rim to the long summit crest of Creise, marked with several cairns (GR238506) (3h). Continue southwards along the ridge for about 600m beyond the last summit cairn to a small cairn on the ridge. [Detour: descend east from here, where a path drops suddenly through crags, with some easy scrambling. Reach a bealach and climb over rocky terrain to the summit of Meall a'Bhùiridh and its mast just beyond. Return to Creise ridge (add 1h40).] From this point, descend WSW along a well-defined ridge to a bealach. Ascend steeper slopes northwest to the summit of Beinn Mhic Chasgaig (GR221502) (4h20). Walk north for about 300m, avoiding the steep east slopes, and then start to descend the grassy NNE ridge. This leads gently down into Glen Etive. Cross the river to reach the road and walk back to the start (5h20).

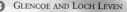

Buachaille Etive Mór

Buachaille Etive Mór:
Stob Dearg ⓜ(1021m), **Stob na Doire**
(1011m), **Stob na Bròige** ⓜ(956m)

Walk time **6h** Height gain **1100m**
Distance **15km** OS Map Explorer 384

**Stob Dearg is a year-round favourite
with climbers and an icon for travellers
passing into Glencoe. This route
includes steep ground to attain and
leave the curving ridge, which makes
it particularly tricky in winter.**

Start from Altnafeadh, 4km northwest of
the Kingshouse Hotel (GR221563). (Park
here or 800m west, at the end of the route.)
Bear south from the houses and cross the
River Coupall by a footbridge. A good path
leads past the cottage of Lagangarbh to a
junction after 200m. Turn right and
continue by a rocky path towards Coire na
Tulaich: this accompanies the burn on the
west side and gains rapid height into the
bowl. The last slopes where the path fades
out are steep (tricky in winter), but soon
lead to the broad rocky ridge at a cairn.
Climb east, following the ridge to the top of
Stob Dearg, the main peak (GR223542).
Descend west back to the cairn. Walk over
a small knoll and then turn southwest.
Descend gently before tackling the
pyramidal Stob na Doire, which provides
fairly steep climbing right to the summit
(GR208533) (3h20). Descend the steep
southwest ridge, keeping to the rocky
ground of the apex to avoid the drop on
both sides: this leads down to a bealach.

From here, climb westwards to the summit of Stob Coire Altruim, which boasts an impressive high buttress on its northern face. Continue southwest for a further 1km over various small knolls to the final top of Stob na Bròige. Descend WSW along the main ridge for about 600m in distance to reach a steep scree chute and broken crags on the north aspect. Descend northwest with care: further down, maintain the height to reach the cairn at the high point of the Lairig Gartain. From here, a boggy path leads you northeast along the River Coupall. After about 4km, this takes you back to the road, close to Altnafeadh (6h).

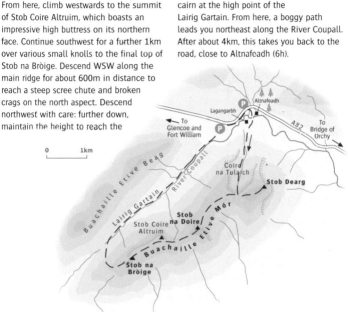

Mountain Rescue

As the popularity of the hills grew after the Second World War, the number of accidents increased. The Mountain Rescue Committee for Scotland was set up in 1950, involving the climbing clubs, the RAF and other bodies. The Glencoe Mountain Rescue Team was established in 1961, with local climbing legend Hamish MacInnes as a founder member. All members of the rescue team are volunteers and funding is entirely dependent on donations. Many accidents occur on descent from the hills when daylight is limited and tiredness leads to mistakes. There are plenty of rescues from the Aonach Eagach, especially when walkers attempt to descend south into Glen Coe. The steep ground on Buachaille Etive Mór and Bidean nam Bian also sees accidents and avalanches.

◀ Buachaille Etive Mór from the Kingshouse Hotel

The Little Shepherd

Buachaille Etive Beag: Stob Dubh ⓜ
(958m), Stob Coire Raineach ⓜ**(925m)**

Walk time **3h40** + detour 40 min
Height gain **800m**
Distance **9km** OS Map Explorer 384

**Compact circuit of two high mountains
above the watershed between Glencoe
and Rannoch Moor. This route involves
some steep stretches in ascent and
descent and one short exposed section.**

Start from the path for Lochetiveside
above the Meeting of Three Waters, the
main falls in Glen Coe (GR187563). (Better
parking 300m east along the road.) This
path leads southwest, soon dropping to
cross and follow the Allt Lairig Eilde. Keep
to the burn for 3km to reach a bealach,
marked with a large cairn, between Stob
Coire Sgreamhach and Stob Dubh
(GR170534). The main path now starts to
descend into Glen Etive: do not follow the
path but leave it to climb east and join the
blunt west ridge of Stob Dubh. This soon
steepens but is never difficult, and it is
possible to keep to grass and boulders and

avoid the scree for most of the journey to the summit (GR179535) (2h40). Descend the northeast ridge, which flattens but has steep drops on either side. The exposure soon eases and the route drops down to a bealach. [Detour: continue to the top of Stob Coire Raineach via its southwest ridge.

Return to the bealach (add 40 min).] Descend NNW along a good but sometimes boggy path to lose altitude quickly. This reaches the original path along the Lairig Eilde. Retrace your steps back to the start point (3h40).

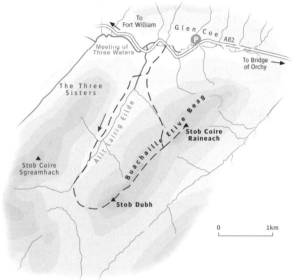

The Massacre

Glencoe is best known for an event that began early on the morning of 13 February 1692 when government troops under the command of Captain Robert Campbell of Glen Lyon rose from the beds provided by their MacDonald hosts to 'put all to the sword under seventy'. The reasons behind the notorious 'murder under trust' are colourfully explained at the National Trust for Scotland Visitor Centre just off the main road.

◄ Buachaille Etive Beag (The Little Shepherd) from Coire na Tulaich

The Lost Valley

Bidean nam Bian ⓜ (1150m),
Stob Coire nan Lochan (1115m)

Walk time **5h** Height gain **1200m**
Distance **10km** OS Map Explorer **384**

A walk over two craggy peaks high above the historic Glen Coe with an interesting approach and return under the Three Sisters. Steep cliffs around Stob Coire nan Lochan make good compass work essential.

Start from one of two large parking areas facing the Three Sisters, west of the sharp bends in the road (GR172568). Cross down to the floor of the glen and head southeast towards the upper of two footbridges, near the Meeting of Three Waters. Cross the River Coe and climb by a good path through boulders and forest, following the Allt Coire Gabhail to emerge above the Lost Valley, a large, flat area with cliffs on all sides which is reputed to have provided a hiding place for clansfolk and their cattle. Descend into the bowl and follow the burn southwest. Further up the valley, where the terrain steepens, climb westwards to a bealach to the south of Stob Coire nan Lochan. Ascend the ridge southwest to the summit of Bidean nam Bian (GR143542) (3h20). Return to the bealach and climb northwards o the top of Stob Coire nan Lochan. Care is required in this area: the cliffs are steep and a favourite with climbers. Descend northwest to join the north ridge down to gentler ground, then bear southeast into the corrie basin. Continue down the steep Coire nan Lochan by a path on the east bank of the burn. This leads to the glen and a bridge a short distance from the road (5h).

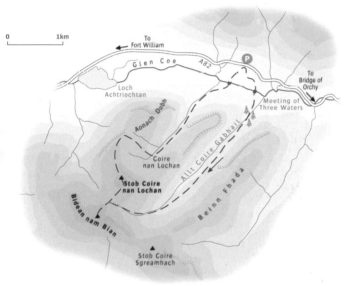

The Holy Grail

'The Glen of Weeping', as Glen Coe is sometimes known, is not without its lighter touches. A narrow gorge near the Meeting of Three Waters was the filming location for the Bridge of Death scene in the comedy classic *Monty Python and the Holy Grail*. Rannoch Moor also features in the film, as does Castle Stalker disguised as Castle Aargh. Constrained by a limited budget and wary property owners, the film-makers also had to employ Doune Castle in different scenes as Swamp Castle, Castle Anthrax and Camelot itself.

◀ Stob Coire nan Lochan from the Meeting of Three Waters

Glencoe's hidden treasure

Sgòr na h-Ulaidh ⑩ (994m),
Stob an Fhuarain (968m)

Walk time **5h40** Height gain **1100m**
Distance **13km** OS Map **Landranger 41**

**Two high peaks reached by good
access tracks and paths with steep
terrain and tricky navigation higher
up. This route returns along a less
frequented glen.**

Start 1km south of the Glencoe Visitor
Centre at a track marked for Gleann-leac-
na-muidhe on the south side of the road
(GR118565). (Parking just east of the
bridge.) Walk along this track for 2.5km,
past houses and through a farm. Further on,
the track becomes a path: follow it on the

east bank of the Allt na Muidhe through a
fine glen dominated by steep cliffs to the
west. Higher up, as the glen widens, cross
the burn and climb southwest towards the
bealach between Meall Lighiche and Corr
na Beinne, marked with iron fencing. Climb
steeply south to Corr na Beinne: there are
cliffs but these can be easily avoided to
reach easier ground. Bear east along a good
ridge to reach the exposed summit of
Sgòr na h-Ulaidh (GR111518) (3h20). The
descent requires some care as the northern
corrie is steep. Walk 100m to the east and
then drop northeast over rocky ground to
reach a bealach, before climbing to the top
of Stob an Fhuarain. Descend southeast
along the pronounced ridge which soon

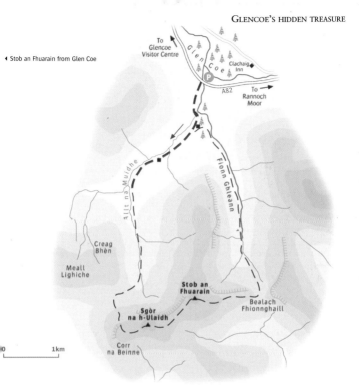

◀ Stob an Fhuarain from Glen Coe

twists to the east. The ridge drops in waves above a crag-lined corrie which lies hidden from Glen Coe. As you approach Bealach Fhionnghaill, where the ground steepens just before the lowest point, take a grassy ramp northwards to reach the corrie floor. Keep to the west bank of the burn which flows through Fionn Ghleann. The water drops suddenly at the start of some fenceposts which lead down the glen. There is no real path but this terrain is never hard

and takes you all of the way down to a plantation and a fence. Pass through the fence by a gate close to the water. Bear west across boggy ground, aiming for the mid-point of two plantations (the upper one sparse, the lower containing a house). Watch for a gate just above the lower plantation. Once through the gate, walk clockwise around the forest and over bumpy ground to reach the original track. Follow this back to the start (5h40).

Aonach Eagach from Loch Leven

Am Bodach (943m), **Meall Dearg** ⓜ
(953m), **Sgorr nam Fiannaidh** ⓜ (967m)

Walk time **9h** Height gain **1300m**
Distance **24km** OS Map Explorer **384**

**This famous ridge involves sustained
scrambling, rock-climbing (rope advised)
and severe exposure. It is very serious
in winter. Take care not to dislodge rock
and keep your distance from other
parties, as this ridge is popular.**

Start at the bridge over the River Leven in
Kinlochleven (GR188619). Walk along a
tarmac road on the south side of the river,
passing the power station, to reach the
West Highland Way. Turn right to follow the
track southwards as it gains height above
the glen. Cross a bridge, and climb until you
reach a pumping station: here, the main
track drops but the West Highland Way

turns right as a wide stony path. Follow this
for 2km until you have climbed steep
zigzags, below Sròn a'Choire Odhair-bhig.
Leave the path at this point and climb
southwest up this grassy ridge: the terrain
eases higher up. Follow this to an unnamed
peak, around the corrie and on to the top of
Sròn Gharbh (GR178584) (4h). [Escape:
descend northeast directly from the
summit, steeply and over awkward terrain
at first. Reach flatter ground and cross the
northern tributary of the Allt Coire Mhorair.
Follow the water to the track.] The character
of the ridge changes dramatically from here.
Descend WSW to a bealach and then climb
the steep east face of Am Bodach by a
rough path to its summit. Descend WNW
along a narrow crest that drops sharply:
many parties use a rope for this initial
section. Scramble down a pillar on the

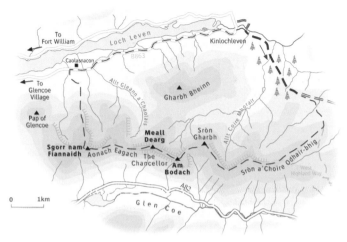

north side before a traverse left to the apex leaves a few moves to safer ground. Continue over the Chancellor on the exposed ridge and climb to the top of Meall Dearg. [Escape: descend north by fenceposts to reach a bealach shared with Gharbh Bheinn. Descend either side: west to join a grassy track to Caolasnacon or east along the Allt Coire Mhorair to meet the track.] The most exhilarating part of the traverse is the next 600m: there is no escape and a rope at certain places is advisable. After a short drop westwards, the first tower eases you in gently with a chimney to ascend and descend; some difficulties can be avoided by traversing on the south side. The Crazy Pinnacles start after the third tower: three rock needles requiring deft scrambling that mark the halfway point. A hard move gains the tower beyond (it is better to stick to the apex rather than any loose options on the

north side). From this point more height is lost than gained, descending rocky steps and threading a clever way through jagged crags. The exposure and difficulties end abruptly, and it's an easy climb up scree to the top of Stob Coire Leith. Continue westwards to the final summit of Sgorr nam Fiannaidh (GR141583) (6h40). Descend northwards over scree: after 500m the terrain steepens over sharp rock and grass. A few craggy parts can be avoided to reach a flat area and small grassy knoll, marked with a cairn. Continue to descend the spur: lower down rocky ribs try to lead you west towards the Pap. Descend northwest before the ridge steepens but as late as possible, as the undergrowth in the corrie is hard to negotiate. Join a small burn and take the path under the pylons to reach the road by a bridge near Caolasnacon. Walk, hitch or catch the bus back to Kinlochleven (9h).

◄ The wild towers of the Aonach Eagach above Glen Coe

The old man of the Mamores

Stob Coire a'Chàirn ⓜ (981m),
An Gearanach ⓜ (982m),
Am Bodach ⓜ (1032m)

Walk time 5h20 + detour 1h20
Height gain 1200m
Distance 12km OS Map Landranger 41

**Several high and rocky peaks of the
Mamores, accessed by good tracks and
paths. Scrambling skills will increase
confidence on this route and are
required for the detour.**

Start at a sign for the West Highland Way
by the school and MacDonald Hotel in
Kinlochleven (GR183623). Take the West
Highland Way, which climbs up through the
trees and shortly reaches a minor road. Turn
right and follow the road as it snakes up to
the Mamore Lodge Hotel. Beyond the hotel,
the road becomes a gravel track and forks
after 100m. Turn right towards the stalker's
cottage: this is bypassed on the south side
by a path which rejoins the track after the
buildings. Follow the track northwards for
another 800m and cross a bridge over the
Allt Coire na Bà. Immediately after the
bridge, leave the gravel track and take a
grassy track that heads north into the glen

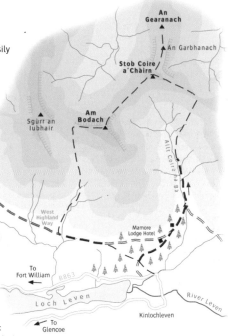

above. This gains height easily
and leads into the corrie
below the bastions of Am
Bodach. In the depths of
the corrie, where the
track ends, start to
climb steeply
northeast by a small
burn to reach a
prominent bealach
between Na
Gruagaichean and
Stob Coire a'Chàirn.
Variant: an old path,
hard to follow in
places, runs east and
then north to gain the
bealach, giving a
longer but easier
ascent.] Climb
northwest along the
ridge to the summit
of Stob Coire a'Chàirn
(GR185661) (3h20). [Detour:
descend NNE to a small bealach
and climb An Garbhanach. This ascent
and the subsequent traverse to the higher
An Gearanach is exposed and involves
scrambling. Return to Stob Coire a'Chàirn
(add 1h20).] Descend southwest with ease
to a bealach before the entertaining and
easy scramble through small, rocky
buttresses to the summit of Am Bodach.
Descend west along a sharp ridge strewn
with cuboid blocks. At the lowest point on
the ridge towards Sgùrr an Iubhair, descend

south to soon find a good path which
hugs the east bank of a burn. Lower down,
this path crosses to the west bank and
meets a wide track shared with the West
Highland Way. Turn left to reach a fork
after 300m. Descend southeast along the
West Highland Way (the track leads to the
hotel), which takes you back to
Kinlochleven (5h20).

◄ The eastern corrie of Am Bodach

39

Ballachulish Horseshoe

Sgorr Dhonuill ⓜ (1001m),
Sgorr Dhearg ⓜ (1024m)

Walk time **7h40** Height gain **1500m**
Distance **18km** OS Map Landranger **41**

**A high, undulating plateau and a rocky
ridge accessed by forestry tracks and
steep open hill. There is a real mix of
terrain on this route, with an exposed
and rocky descent.**

Start at the entrance to the Glenachulish
Forest in South Ballachulish (GR046587).
Follow an excellent track south towards the
cirque of Beinn a'Bheithir. At the first
intersection, continue straight on along the
tarmac road that gains height on the west
side of the glen. Pass a minor turn to the
left and continue to the more significant
junction 300m from the bridge. Turn right,
and follow a gravel track that rises
northwards in fits and starts around the
ridge. After 2km, at a gate by a pebble-
dashed building with a mast, the track exits

the forest. Climb over the gate and start to
ascend grassy slopes southwards, just to the
right of a burn. Higher up, the ground
becomes more complex with crags and
boulder-filled dips. Keep about 100m west
of a large rocky nose for the easiest line
and continue to the plateau, where the
cirque and the high buttresses of Sgorr
Dhonuill come into view. You soon reach
the first top, marked with south-facing
slabs. This fine but seldom-visited ridge
curves in a gentle mirrored-S with several
dips and bumps. After 3km, easy-angled
slopes lead east to the summit of Sgorr
Dhonuill (GR040555) (4h40). Descend the
east ridge, at first through broken rocks
before the terrain eases, to reach a bealach.
Climb northeast to the summit of Sgorr
Dhearg, where sits the sorry remains of a
trig point. Descend the fine north ridge. This
begins with steep rock steps with some
exposure, as the sides of the spur are steep.
Further down, as you approach wider grassy

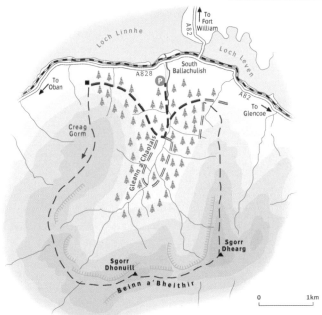

slopes, the difficulties recede. Reach a low fence and cross by a stile before starting a northwest descent off the ridge. This bearing leads you into a harvested area of the Glenachulish plantation. The stumps and folded ground are awkward to navigate,

so choose your route with care and aim to reach the forest tracks at a junction. Take the lower track that leads southwards to the bridge across the burn. This gives access to the original track: it is just a short distance to the start (7h40).

The Appin murder

The cairn at the south end of Ballachulish Bridge commemorates James Stewart, 'James of the Glens', cruelly and wrongly executed for the murder in Appin, Argyll in 1752 of Colin Campbell of Glenure, King's Factor of forfeited Jacobite estates. Although Robert Louis Stevenson made Jacobite adventurer Alan Breck Stewart the possible assassin in his fiction *Kidnapped*, the real culprit is said to be known only within certain local families, the name passed down from father to son on their coming of age.

◀ Beinn a'Bheithir from Onich

41

Fort William is the largest town of the central and western Highlands and, with mountains and deep lochs on almost all sides, the hub for adventure sport in the region. Rising above the town, Ben Nevis has been a favourite with mountaineers for over a century and hosts some of Scotland's finest climbing routes. The Nevis Range at Aonach Mór has skiing and some great mountain biking: the annual world championships are held here in early summer. Fort William is well served by accommodation, with over a mile of hotels and guesthouses on the southern approach along Loch Linnhe and plenty more room in town. The quieter Glen Spean hides a series of small villages yet is still well connected to Fort William by rail and road.

These routes include some of Scotland's highest peaks, but there are also easier walks in the area. 'The Ben' is climbed with its neighbour Carn Mór Dearg to form a large horseshoe; two routes on the Mamores are tackled from Glen Nevis; and the Aonachs are ascended with help from the Nevis Range ski gondola. Two long routes on the Grey Corries begin in Spean Bridge, one of which is best accessed by mountain bike. Glen Roy, with its unusual geological legacy, hosts two shorter routes.

Glen Nevis and Glen Spean

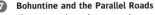

The Ben from Fort William

Carn Mór Dearg ⓜ (1220m),
Ben Nevis ⓜ (1344m)

Walk time 7h40 Height gain 1500m
Distance 17km OS Map Explorer 392

This circuit allows you to admire the rugged cliffs of the Ben before tackling the summit. An intricate start and a difficult descent, particularly in bad weather, make sharp navigation essential. The summit plateau is often corniced into summer.

Start at Fort William railway station. Walk through the supermarket car park, and turn right onto the road at the entrance. Pass the Nevis Centre to reach a playground and Camanachd Crescent after 400m. Turn left along the crescent to reach a bridge on the right after 160m. Cross the bridge and turn left to follow a path along the River Lochy. After 1300m the path joins a track. Turn left

and pass under the railway bridge to reach Inverlochy Castle. From the front of the castle, walk northeast by the river to reach the road junction at the Ben Nevis Distillery (40 min). (No parking without permission.) Cross the road and walk through the distillery grounds, keeping left with the Still House on your right to find a gap on the left just after Cask Shed No1. Go through the gap, and turn right to follow a path under the railway and out to open ground. This reaches a track after 500m. Turn left on the track and walk northeast, crossing two footbridges to gain the signposted path along the Allt a'Mhuilinn. (This can also be reached from the North Face car park at Torlundy.) Follow the path, rising steeply southeast through birch to emerge at a track. Continue straight on, arching right at the next junction to reach a stile into open ground. Beyond the stile, follow the path

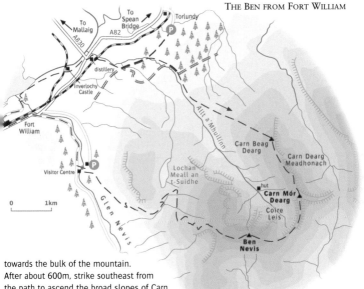

towards the bulk of the mountain. After about 600m, strike southeast from the path to ascend the broad slopes of Carn Beag Dearg. This is tiring, but once on the arête height is maintained for the day. The views across to Ben Nevis' northern corries and buttresses are fantastic, especially in winter when the huge wall of Orion Face and the numbered gullies assume an alpine feel. Continue easily along the ridge to Carn Dearg Meadhonach and the summit of Carn Mór Dearg (GR177702) (4h40). Care should be taken on the rest of the route due to the steep terrain: large cornices may also form in winter. Descend south along the ridge, with steep ground on either side, to a bealach above Coire Leis. [Escape: drop steeply on the northern side into Coire Leis to the locked CIC hut, and follow the east bank of the Allt a'Mhuilinn.] Climb southwest then northwest, keeping the

crest of the ridge to the summit plateau of Ben Nevis (GR167713) (5h40). The descent from the old observatory is very particular: the vast plateau has steep cliffs on **both** sides and has caused many accidents; take bearings and pace out distances. Follow these **grid** bearings for a safe descent: 231° for 150m, then 281° for 1500m. Follow the broad scree-covered flanks northwest towards Lochan Meall an t-Suidhe and level ground. Take the zigzag path southwest and then northwest into Glen Nevis. Just before Achintee House, take a path that leads down to the River Nevis. Cross the river by a footbridge close to the visitor centre, and follow the road back into town (7h40).

◀ Ben Nevis from Loch Eil

45

The Devil's Ridge

Sgùrr a'Mhaim ⓜ(1099m), **Sgòr an Iubhair** (1001m), **Stob Bàn** ⓜ(999m), **Mullach nan Coirean** ⓜ(939m)

Walk time 7h20 Height gain 1600m
Distance 13km OS Map Landranger 41

Great ridge walk in the Mamores with plenty of excitement in the form of a steep climb to start, some exposure and scrambling, and a forest adventure to complete the circuit.

Start from Achriabhach in Glen Nevis, where there is a long bridge that crosses both the Water of Nevis and the smaller Allt Coire a'Mhusgain (GR145683). (Large car park here.) Between the two rivers, there is a stile on the east side: climb this to follow a path through an open field. This path shadows the Allt Coire a'Mhusgain into the higher glen. After about 1km, leave the main path for a vague trail that ascends

the blunt northwest ridge of Sgùrr a'Mhaim. This is steep with frequent switches to gain height quickly, but it is a punishing 1000m climb. A vast scree pile caps the mountain and provides some interest before you reach the summit of Sgùrr a'Mhaim. Descend south by a steep path. This joins the Devil's Ridge, a narrow and exposed journey with fine views on both sides. There are two tops on the ridge, with some easy scrambling: the hardest moves are on leaving the low point between the two tops. The ridge leads to easier ground from which it is a short climb to the summit of Sgòr an Iubhair (GR165655) (3h20). Descend southwest, keeping clear of hidden crags to the west of the summit. The west ridge then leads down to a bealach near a lochan, a fine place for a stop. Continue west to the summit of Stob Bàn: although steep, it is easier than it looks and gives some

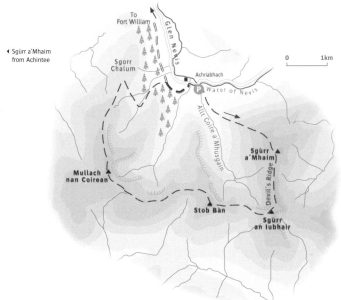

◀ Sgùrr a'Mhaim
from Achintee

exposure over its rocky northern corrie.
Descend NNW from the top towards an
outlying knoll. This can be bypassed on the
south, with gentle walking along the rest of
the ridge. Continue westwards over two
small craggy knolls, with their needles and
pinnacles, before tackling Mullach nan
Coirean: this offers no difficulties to reach
the summit (GR122662) (6h). Descend
northwards and take the blunt north ridge
rather than the eroded northeast spur. This
entertaining ridge dips and flattens in
waves: follow it for 2.5km to reach a hollow
with a fence and stile before the craggy
knoll of Sgorr Chalum. Rather than cross

the stile, follow the plantation fence
southeast over heathery slopes to drop
steeply into Coire Riabhach. Lower down,
ignore a gate in the fence and descend to
the burn. Ford the water to reach a stile on
the other side after 100m. Cross this stile,
and make your way along a rough path that
twists through birch and occasional deep
mud. This path improves as it enters thick
forest and then drops rightwards by steps to
a gravel track. Turn right along the track
and walk for about 800m to a switchback.
Watch for the waymarked forest trail, which
descends through the trees by the burn and
back into Glen Nevis (7h20).

A Glen Nevis trek

Sgùrr Eilde Mór ⓜ(1010m),
Na Gruagaichean ⓜ(1056m),
Binnein Mór ⓜ(1130m),
Binnein Beag ⓜ(943m)

Walk time 9h + detours 1h40
Height gain 1300m
Distance 23km OS Map Landranger 41

**Long route over multiple tops reached
on good access paths from Glen Nevis,
Glen Spean or Corrour Station. There are
steep descents, a short section of
scrambling and a river crossing. This
would be a harder undertaking in winter.**

Start at the car park at the end of the
public road in Glen Nevis (GR167691). Walk
eastwards by the path from the end of the
road, overlooking the fast-flowing Water of
Nevis. This takes you past a wire bridge, the
Steall Hut and ruins to reach Tom an Eite at
the watershed (GR238694). Cross to the
south side of the Allt Coire a'Bhinnein here,
and climb the rolling heather of Meall Doire
na h-Achlais. This forms the northeast ridge
of Sgùrr Eilde Mór, and from here easier
terrain can be followed to the summit
(GR230658) (4h40). Descend due west
along a narrow ridge. A steep path stays
close to the apex, mostly on its northern
side, and leads down to the north side of
the Coire an Lochain. Skirt around the
lochan, climb up the other side and cross a
wide north-south path. Instead of taking
this, continue west along a small path. This

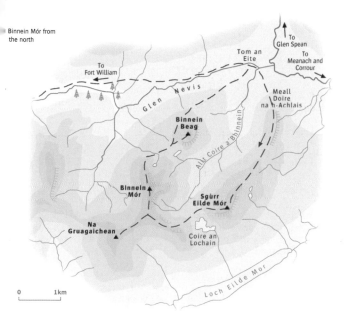

Binnein Mór from the north

To Glen Spean

To Meanach and Corrour

Tom an Eite

To Fort William

Glen Nevis

Meall Doire na h-Achlais

Binnein Beag

Allt Coire a'Bhinnein

Binnein Mór

Sgúrr Eilde Mór

Na Gruagaichean

Coire an Lochain

0   1km

Loch Eilde Mór

rises gently to climb the north flanks of Sgor Eilde Beag and then zigzags close to some prominent slabs, emerging on the ridge by a cairn. Follow the ridge WNW to an unnamed top with cairn and grassy knoll. [Detour: descend southwest by a rocky ridge to a bealach, before climbing to the summit of Na Gruagaichean (GR203652). Return the same way (add 1h).] From the knoll, bear due north, dropping slightly before climbing to the summit of Binnein Mór (GR212663) (6h20). Scramble steeply down over trickier and exposed rocky ground on the NNW to join the north ridge, and then follow this until it flattens out and it is easy to traverse east to a bealach and lochan. [Detour: taken from the south, the summit of Binnein Beag is a short climb. Return to the lochan (add 40min).] Locate a path that skirts the western side of Binnein Beag. Once around the peak, continue to descend northeast over grassy slopes to the glen. Cross the river to reach the path on the north side: return west to Glen Nevis (9h) or east to Meanach and Corrour.

Traverse of the Aonachs

Aonach Mór ⓜ(1221m), **Aonach Beag**
(1234m), **Sgùrr Chòinnich Mór** ⓜ(1094m),
Stob Coire Easain (1080m),
Stob Coire an Laoigh ⓜ (1116m)

Walk time **9h** + detour **40 min**
Height gain **1200m** Distance **24km**
OS Map Landranger **41**

**Long day out that takes in a number of
high peaks with one section of steep
descent and a return by bike tracks. This
route can be particularly demanding in
winter. Stamina is essential.**

Start from the Nevis Range ski station
(GR172774). (There is a regular bus service
from Fort William.) Take the gondola to the
top station by Sgùrr Finnisg-aig. On exit
from the station, climb southeast towards
the rockier eastern ridge of Aonach an Nid,
passing a complex system of ski fences.
This leads past the highest ski tow where
the ridge becomes quite sharp. Continue
SSW more easily and follow the edge of the

steep corrie to reach a small cairn. About
1km of much flatter ground leads to the
summit plateau of Aonach Mór with its
large cairn. Continue south, dropping gently
over grass to a bealach, after which the
terrain changes. The climb to the summit of
Aonach Beag is quickly completed
(GR196715) (2h40). Descend south over
interesting terrain, watching for the steep
cliffs on the eastern corrie which cut
suddenly into the ridge. The ridge then
turns southeast, descending over bumps
and dips to reach Stob Coire Bhealaich.
Drop down on the south side to reach a
small cairn just below the top. The descent
directly east is not recommended: instead
traverse southwest, keeping above the
corrie rim, and down to a rocky bealach
shared with Sgùrr a'Bhiuc. Continue to the
far end of the bealach and find a steep
grassy runnel on the east side. Once you
have reached easy ground below, traverse
northeast over complex terrain to return to

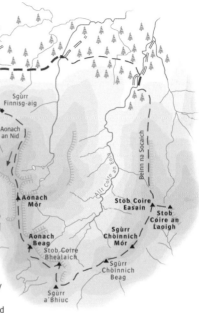

◀ The Aonachs from Inverroy

the main ridge. Climb eastwards to the top of Sgùrr Chòinnich Beag, and Sgùrr Chòinnich Mór just beyond (GR227714) (5h). Here, the ridge gains more definition, leading northeast with one rocky step to flatter ground. The rocky south ridge of Stob Coire Easain is entertaining and easier than it looks. [Detour: drop ESE to a bealach and climb to the summit of Stob Coire an Laoigh before returning the same way (add 40 min.).] From the summit cairn, continue east for about 50m and descend easily along the north ridge. Follow the ridge over Beinn na Socaich and down across easy grass slopes for 3km. Further down, the birch-covered slopes on the west side overlook a set of great waterfalls. Continue on the ridge until it is easy to drop west into the corrie, where a dirt track leads down to the Allt Coire an Eoin. The track doubles back to follow the river to a gate and bridge. Pass through the gate, and continue down an excellent track to reach a dilapidated railway bridge after 500m. Leave the track here and ford the river (but don't use the bridge) to find the line of the old railway on the other side. [Variant: the

river is normally low as it is diverted for water supplies, but if in spate continue to a bridge 2.5km north.] The start of the railway is boggy, but soon joins a mountain bike track. From this point the route is shared with mountain bikers, who take priority. Follow the upper track at the next two junctions, past freshly harvested forest. After a zigzag descent, take a wide track west over the river. This climbs slightly and levels out for 2km to reach a junction within sight of the gondola cables. Turn left at the junction and, after 200m, take the mountain bike trail on the right. This leads back to the start (9h).

Over the Grey Corries

Stob Coire Gaibhre (958m),
Stob Choire Claurigh Ⓜ(1177m),
Caisteil (1106m)

Walk time **8h40** Height gain **1300m**
Distance **24km** OS Map **Landranger 41**

**A long route which approaches through
forest to attain a snaking ridge with
several entertaining peaks. The terrain
is rocky and complex but never difficult.**

Start from the Spean Bridge Hotel in
Spean Bridge (GR222815). Just south of the
hotel, take the minor road east to follow
the River Spean. After 3km, a track leads
south to the farm at Corriechoille. Take this
track past the house and through farmland
to reach a plantation at a gate. Enter the
forest, and climb up through The Lairig to
emerge from the trees after 1.5km.
Continue along the track for about 200m
until an enclosed area on the right gives
way to open ground. Turn west off the track
to cross boggy terrain within sight of Ruigh
na Gualainn, the steep and broken crags to
the south. After 500m, bear south again
over undulating ground which becomes
firmer the higher you climb. This leads to
the top of Stob Coire Gaibhre. Descend

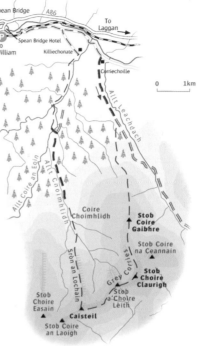

slightly and continue south for 1.5km to a minor bump. The main ridge of the Grey Corries corkscrews ahead. Climb south to the summit of Stob Choire Claurigh, where the ridge becomes narrow and rocky but never exposed (GR262738) (5h). This peak affords good views over the steep cliffs of the next peak, Stob a'Choire Lèith, which is reached easily over a terrain of scree and small boulders. Continue over Stob Coire Cath na Sine and on to Caisteil. At this top, begin a descent along Sròn an Lochain, the prominent north ridge. Lower down this loses definition, but continue northwards into Coire Choimhlidh over grassy slopes – keeping to the east side of the Allt Choimhlidh to reach a dam at the start of the forest. A gate gives access to a track which shadows the burn. Follow this north, ignoring turns on either side until you reach a small bridge over the Allt Coire an Eoin after 2km. A path on the other side leads north to Killiechonate. Turn left at the first house, then continue straight on to reach the original road back to Spean Bridge (8h40).

On yer bike

Aonach Mór plays host to Britain's longest downhill mountain bike track, with a 600m drop. This route is not for the faint-hearted: riders use front and rear suspension and full body armour. Aonach Mór first hosted the World Championships in 2002. Originally developed as the Nevis Range ski area it has diversified to ensure year-round employment and popularity.

◀ The Grey Corries from Loch Lochy

53

Hidden glens of Lochaber

Stob Ban Ⓜ (977m)

Walk time **6h40** Height gain **1100m**
Approach and return **2h bike or 5h walk**
Distance **18km** + 18km approach and
return OS Map Landranger 41

**One high peak combined with a tour of
several remote glens on a network of
good paths. This long route is best
accessed by mountain bike.**

Start from the Spean Bridge Hotel in
Spean Bridge (GR222815). Just south of the
hotel, take the minor road east to follow
the River Spean. After 3km, a track leads
south to the farm at Corriechoille. Take this
track past the house and through farmland
to reach a plantation at a gate. Enter the
forest and climb up through The Lairig to
emerge after 1.5km. Cross the Allt
Leachdach and keep to the track as it
follows the burn through the steep-sided
glen. Drop over the bealach and continue
down to the Leacach Bothy (GR282736).
Mountain bikes are best left here: walk
times start from this point. Head south on a
path, and watch for a right turning after
about 400m. Begin to climb southwest over
boggy and undulating ground. After
flattening out at mid-height, the last 500m
steepens sharply to the summit of Stob Ban
(GR267724) (1h20). Descend southwest
along the gently sloping ridge to a bealach
shared with Meall a'Bhùirich. Instead of
climbing this top, descend southeastwards,
easily bypassing a few rocky steps and
small waterfalls, to join an excellent path

that heads southwards down to the Meanach Bothy (GR266685), a welcome shelter in this isolated glen. Follow the river on its meandering course downstream, passing a series of waterfalls and the Staoineag Bothy on the opposite bank. The burn flows to Loch Treig at the ramshackle Creaguaineach Lodge (GR309689) (4h40).

Turn north and follow the Allt na Lairige on its west bank as it passes through a steep ravine. The glen opens up beyond and climbs slowly, passing more waterfalls, through the Lairig Leacach and back to the first bothy (6h40). Follow the same route back to Glen Spean: this is a terrific ride for cyclists.

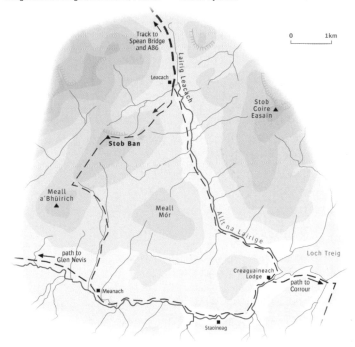

◀ Glen Spean and the Leannachan Forest from the south

Bohuntine and the Parallel Roads

Beinn a'Mhonicag (Bohuntine) (567m)

Walk time **3h20** Height gain **400m**
Distance **7km** OS Map Landranger 41

Half-day out on a great peak with a steep climb to start, rough walking and plenty of geological interest.

Start from the viewpoint and car park in Glen Roy, 6km northeast of Roybridge (GR297853). Climb due west up the steep grassy slopes of Bohuntine directly from the parking area. The route cuts over the famous Parallel Roads, which now feel much less of a landmark than they look from a distance. The angle does not diminish until you reach the summit plateau of Bohuntine and its three cairns (GR287854) (1h). Descend southwest along an undulating ridge until you reach a fence, then descend northwest into Caol

Lairig over steep and awkward slopes of heather. Keep a line roughly aiming for the plantation on the other side of the glen to reach the Allt Coire Ionndrainn. Follow animal trails upstream through this secretive glen. Further up, a school of whale-like moraines shelter a few birch trees where several small tributaries meet. Climb the most central of these moraines and walk northwards over the heather to join a good track after 200m. This can be followed east to give easy walking. The track keeps level at first before dropping steeply down to the road above Glen Roy by Achavady, an old ruin. Walk south back to the start (3h20).

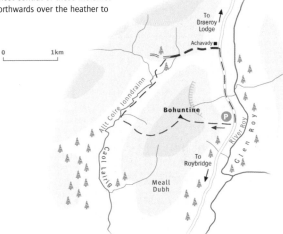

Parallel Roads of Glen Roy

The three parallel 'roads' that can be seen extending along both sides of Glen Roy are the legacy of a unique glacial feature of world importance. Early legend describes how the roads were constructed by Fingal for deer-hunting by chariot, and it was only much later that geologists unravelled the real story. During the ice age, Glen Roy was part of a huge glacial loch with a dam of ice that stretched to Glen Spean. The roads were the original shorelines of the loch, each recording the water level of different periods as temperatures changed.

◀ Glen Roy and its Parallel Roads

Cooling off at Dog Falls

Carn Dearg ⓖ (834m)

Walk time **5h** Height gain **600m**
Distance **13km** OS Map **Landranger 34**

**Steep heathery slopes to climb one
rounded peak of the Monadh Liath.
The route descends over boggy ground
to reach fine waterfalls, and returns
by good paths and tracks.**

Start at the end of the public road in Glen
Roy, at the entrance to the Braeroy Estate
(GR334912). (Limited parking here.) Walk
southwest along the road for 400m to a
bridge and cross the River Roy. Pass the
shed and negotiate your way through a
series of sheep gates and pens to reach a
burn which issues from Coire na Reinich.

Cross to the south side of the water and
follow it upstream. After about 500m, leave
the burn and start to climb southwards
along a vague grassy ridge. Bear eastwards
higher up: the final heather slopes lead to
the undulating plateau of Carn Bhrunachain.
Descend gently ESE to a boggy bealach
before the last climb to the summit of Carn
Dearg and its rocky spine (GR345887)
(2h20). Descend northeast along the ridge
which soon loses its definition. Drop
eastwards to continue over flatter, boggy
terrain. After crossing a fence, bear
northeast over the long boggy slopes above
the Allt Tarsuinn to reach the Dog Falls. The
many waterfalls and deep rock pools, worn
into fantastic shapes, are definitely worth

◀ Dog Falls on the Burn of Agie

the visit. Return to Glen Roy by the path on the west bank of the Burn of Agie. This gains gradual height and switches westwards over a ridge before dropping into the glen. Here, the path fords the Canal Burn and crosses grassland to reach the farm at Annat. Join a track from the farm to the River Roy and follow it downstream, crossing the river by a roadbridge after 1km. The track leads through the estate and back to the start (5h).

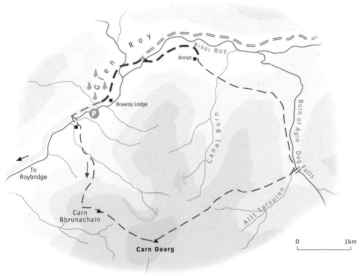

Water

The human body is approximately 70% water. During strenuous exercise, such as walking up steep hills with a rucksack, the body can lose as much as two litres per hour through sweat. Small regular quantities of water are much more beneficial and a readily accessible water bottle, as well as sodium (in salt) to replace lost electrolytes for longer journeys, is crucial. In the Highlands, most natural running water sources are clean, so long as they are not standing or below human activity. If in doubt, use your eyes and nose to investigate.

The West Highland line over the wilderness of Rannoch Moor is one of the world's great rail journeys, even if the trains are now diesel rather than steam powered. As well as providing access for walkers into the lonely hills that surround the moor, residents of the villages around Loch Rannoch use the train, and connecting postbuses, to do their shopping in Fort William. At the head of Glen Spean, the rail meets the road and, here, Loch Laggan leads you east into the untamed massifs of the Monadh Liath and Ardverikie.

Three circuits use the line to start or return, and require some planning: one walk begins at Rannoch Station and ends at Corrour; two routes start at Corrour and go north to Tulloch, one tackling the peaks on the east of Loch Treig, the other the high Easain ridge above the west shore. Another route circles Loch Ossian: this begins and ends at Corrour Station where there are also two welcoming hostels. The other routes in this section are accessed from the road along Loch Laggan. One circuit takes in a pair of peaks above the dam; further east the reclusive Beinn a'Chlachair massif is more easily approached by mountain bike. The National Nature Reserve at Creag Meagaidh contains a fine horseshoe above steep cliffs, and a final route near the village of Laggan ventures into the Monadh Liath.

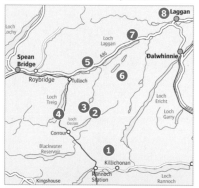

Laggan and Corrour

Rannoch rail trail

Carn Dearg ⓜ (941m), Sgòr Gaibhre ⓜ (955m), Sgòr Choinnich (929m)

Walk time 7h20 Height gain 1100m
Distance 24km
OS Maps Landranger 41 and 42

Exhilarating trek with firm terrain and no real difficulties or steep ascent. This route returns by the Highland Line between Rannoch and Corrour stations. Check rail times before setting out.

Start from a parking bay 2km east of Rannoch Station (GR446578). Take the track known as the Road to the Isles northwards to reach a bridge over the Allt Eigheach after 3km. Cross the water, and continue north on the west bank. The track soon starts to gain height. Follow it to a junction about 1km after the bridge: take the right fork and climb north on the grassy track. When this track turns east to descend into the glen, leave it to continue north over heathery slopes towards the top of Sròn Leachd a'Chaorainn. The ridge undulates north with small outcrops and perched blocks: follow it to reach the summit of Carn Dearg (GR417662) (3h40). [Escape: if running late for the train, descend northwest for 600m and then take the west ridge.] Descend northeast over scree and grass to the bealach of Màm Bàn. From here, it is a steady climb to the summit of Sgòr Gaibhre. The eastern aspect is steep: keep NNW on descent to reach a bealach and then climb steeply north to the top of Sgòr Chòinnich, the final difficulty of the day (GR443683) (5h20). Descend WNW along a prominent ridge and then rise gently to Meall Nathrach Mór, a small knoll. Descend west along the ridge and, when the terrain steepens, drop southwest to the Allt a'Choire Chreagaich towards the plantations. A weir can be easily crossed to reach a track on the opposite bank. Follow the track down through the forest to a collection of estate buildings. Take a left turn after these to find yourself on a track that runs along the south shore

of Loch Ossian. Follow this through the rhododendrons, past the youth hostel and down to Corrour Station. Take the train to Rannoch and walk or catch the postbus to the start (7h20).

Rannoch Moor

'A wearier looking desert man never saw' is how Robert Louis Stevenson described Rannoch Moor in his novel *Kidnapped*. This vast blanket bog no doubt provided good cover for fleeing Jacobites but many have underestimated the dangers of the Moor, not least a group of esteemed railway engineers in January 1889 who, disoriented and exhausted by the sudden onset of bad weather, were very fortunate to be led to safety by local shepherds.

◄ The north ridge of Carn Dearg

Return to Corrour

Beinn na Lap ⑩(935m)

Walk time **6h20** Height gain **600m**
Distance **20km**
OS Maps **Landranger 41 and 42**

**One peak accessed from the Highland
Line. It's a good idea to take trainers
for the long approach around Loch
Ossian. Check train times before setting
out or arrange a stay at one of the
remote Corrour hostels.**

Start from Corrour Station (GR356664).
Take the track east, which passes a junction
after 1km and the youth hostel at Loch
Ossian beyond. Continue past the hostel by
a rough track, which gives fine and easy
walking along the south side of the loch
and later through the rhododendrons of the
Corrour Estate. At the first buildings, bear
northwards to cross the bridge and head for
the recently rebuilt Corrour Lodge. Pass
anti-clockwise around the lodge to reach
another junction by a thatched boathouse.
Turn right to follow the dirt track first north
and then west under the cliffs of Sròn nan
Nead. After 3km, the track reaches a bridge
and turns east. Leave it here to follow a
grassy track along the south bank of the
burn. The track soon forks: turn right and
continue for about 500m. At a convenient
point, leave this track and start to climb
southwest along the defined ridge of Sròn
na Cloiche Sgoilte: there are many false
tops, particularly on the rocky upper
section, but this leads directly to the
summit of Beinn na Lap and several

◄ Looking west along Loch Ossian

shelters (GR376696) (5h). Descend by the undulating southwest ridge. After about 1.5km the spur loses its definition and the slopes ease. At a suitable point, drop south off the ridge, aiming for the head of Loch Ossian. If you hit the deer fence, follow it westwards to a corner: this is then very close to the dirt track on the north side of the loch. Follow this track south to join your original approach, close to the Highland Line (6h20).

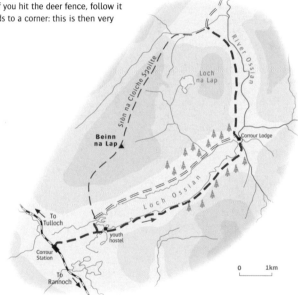

Loch Ossian Youth Hostel

Opened as a hostel in 1931, this former boathouse was one of the first operated by the Scottish Youth Hostels Association (SYHA). Recently refurbished, the remote hostel now has an advanced eco-friendly structure, renewable energy and ecologically sound water and waste disposal systems which take into account the fragile local environment.

Next stop Tulloch

Chno Dearg ⓜ(1046m),
Stob Coire Sgriodain ⓜ(979m)

Walk time **7h40** Height gain **900m**
Distance **22km** OS Map **Landranger 41**

High ridge walk that climbs several
peaks from Rannoch Moor over a variety
of terrain. This route is reached via the
West Highland Line to the remote
Corrour Station. Don't miss your stop.

Start at Corrour Station (GR356664). Walk
northwest along the boggy path that runs
parallel to the railway line until you reach
the foot and railway bridges over the Allt
Luib Ruairidh. Cross the footbridge and turn
off the path to pass beneath the railway
bridge. Begin to climb north up heather
slopes, soon joining a rocky and undulating
ridge which leads northeastwards to the top
of Garbh-bheinn. Drop slightly to climb
Meall Garbh before descending northwards
to a wide bealach with occasional erratics.
Climb northeast to the flat summit of Chno
Dearg (GR377741) (4h). This peak gives
spectacular views of Lochan na h-Earba and
the remote peaks which feed the River
Pattack. Retrace your steps to the bealach,
and bear first westwards and then
northwest over complex and undulating
ground to attain the summit of Stob Coire
Sgriodain with its views over Loch Treig.
Descend northwards for 1km, turning small
buttresses. Keep to the east side of the
ridge to drop down by a grass gully to the
foot of the crags of Sròn na Garbh-bheinne.
Bear east to reach a burn and follow this

Corrour Station

At the highest point on the West
Highland Line from Glasgow to Fort
William and Mallaig, Corrour is
Britain's most isolated rail station.
The builders of the line chose a
different route to the road-builders
and as a result there is no way to
reach it other than by foot or rail.
A great youth hostel is nearby,
however, and the station platform
also houses a comfortable
bunkhouse and a tearoom.
Film fans may recognise the
station from a scene in
Trainspotting.

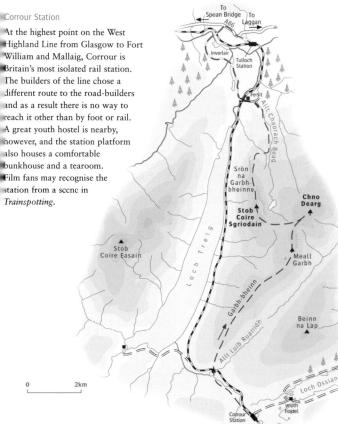

north: ignore the first burn which leads west
and descend north by the rapids of the Allt
Chaorach Beag for some distance to meet
an old track. Follow this north to another
track, and accompany this west for 300m to
join a gravel road close to a farm. Continue
west into Fersit, and follow the minor road
north to Inverlair and out to the A86. Walk
east for 1km and then take the minor road
down to Tulloch Station (7h40).

◄ Stob Coire Sgriodain from Tulloch

67

An Easain adventure

**Stob Coire Easain Ⓜ (1115m),
Stob a'Choire Mheadhoin Ⓜ (1105m)**

Walk time **8h20** Height gain **1000m**
Distance **24km** OS Map **Landranger 41**

**Two mountains and a magnificent ridge
above Loch Treig, reached by a train
journey to Corrour Station. This route
contains some steep ascent and limited
exposure: a harder challenge in winter.**

Start at Corrour Station (GR356664). Walk
northwest along the boggy path that runs
parallel to the railway line. This crosses
several burns, becomes a track and
eventually reaches the shores of Loch Treig.
Continue on the south side of the loch and
cross the Abhainn Rath to reach
Creaguaineach Lodge (GR309689). A path
continues northwards along the loch for
about 400m: follow this and then cross the

Easan Dubh by the bridge. Another path on
the east side of the burn winds along the
steep banks of the ravine before entering an
upper glen. At this point, leave the flats and
make a diagonal northwards ascent of
awkward slopes towards a bealach west of
Creagan a'Chaise. Now ascend steep slopes
to gain the long north-south ridge that
defines the Easains. The ridge is steep-sided
for the next 5km and may be corniced in
winter, providing some exposure. The
climbing eases towards the summit of Stob
Coire Easain (GR308730). Descend
northeast, avoiding the precarious
northwest corrie, to the summit of Stob
a'Choire Mheadhoin (5h40). The ridge drops
gently to the northeast, levelling and falling
again, and gives a steep descent as you
weave through the broken rock
buttresses at Meall Cian Dearg

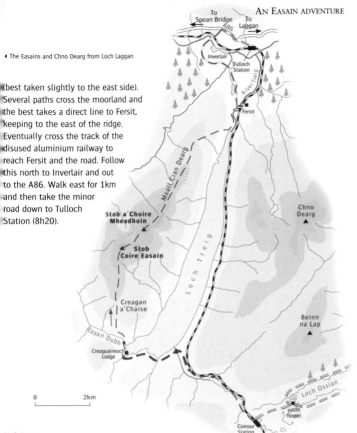

◄ The Easains and Chno Dearg from Loch Laggan

(best taken slightly to the east side). Several paths cross the moorland and the best takes a direct line to Fersit, keeping to the east of the ridge. Eventually cross the track of the disused aluminium railway to reach Fersit and the road. Follow this north to Inverlair and out to the A86. Walk east for 1km and then take the minor road down to Tulloch Station (8h20).

Kelpies

Probably the most feared creatures to inhabit Highland folklore, kelpies or *each-uisge* (water horses) lured travellers onto their backs before riding into the water and drowning them. The most well-known lochs for these beasts are Achtriachtan in Glencoe, Ness, Awe and Coruisk on Skye, but according to legend the most horrible one lives deep in Loch Treig. If you come across it, make sure you have a bridle to hand which you can slip over its head as this is the only way to render it powerless.

Loch Laggan twins

Beinn a'Chaorainn ⓜ (1049m),
Beinn Teallach ⓜ (915m)

Walk time **6h40** Height gain **1200m**
Distance **16km**
OS Map **Landranger 41 or 34**

**Two craggy peaks with views over
Loch Treig. This walk involves plenty
of ascent and an exposed ridge which
is liable to cornicing in winter. It returns
by forest tracks, with one river crossing.**

Start by the picnic bench and gate just
east of Roughburn, overlooking Loch Laggan
(GR377813). (Parking nearby.) Take the track
northwest and then east through the
plantation, climbing gently, and ignoring a
turning on the left after 1km. After another
1km, the track comes to a fence with gate
and stile. Cross the stile and rather than
follow the track beyond, turn to climb
northwards along a vague path through the
forest break. This reaches a gate through
the outer plantation fence after 400m. Pass
through the gate and bear northeast across
uneven moorland towards the upper of two
symmetrical, whale-backed knolls. Follow a
burn from the north until you are above the
knolls on the south ridge of Beinn
a'Chaorainn. This ridge can be followed over
grass and scree, hugging the edge of the
corrie higher up. The south top with its
pointed cairn is attained first. Continue
north to reach the central and main summit

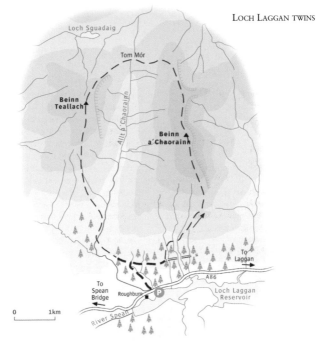

of Beinn a'Chaorainn (GR386851) (3h). Care should be taken on the ridge as the eastern corries are very steep with large cornices tending to build up in winter. Descend to the north and climb to the plateau that constitutes the north top. Descend northwestwards over alternating moss and grass to reach the boggy flats of Tom Mór [Escape: walk south along the glen to follow the Allt a'Chaorainn down to lower tracks.] Climb west over steep heathery slopes to gain an entertaining ridge strewn with boulders and slabs. This leads to the summit of Beinn Teallach with its two tops

(GR362859) (4h40). Descend southwards over gentle and often boggy slopes to reach the corner of a plantation. Jump the rusting fence and follow the edge of the forest to reach a stile. Ford the river just beyond this. [Variant: if the river is in spate, you may need to walk upstream to cross.] Follow a vague path towards a second plantation, and cross the fence by a stile. This leads to a track which enters the forest. Follow the track through the plantation for 1km to reach an intersection with the original access track. Turn right to return to the start (6h40).

Beinn a'Chlachair Circuit

Beinn a'Chlachair ⓜ(1087m),
Geal Charn ⓜ(1049m),
Creag Pitridh (924m)

Walk time **6h** Height gain **1300m**
Approach and return **1h20 bike or 2h40
walk** Distance **14km + 10km approach
and return** OS Map **Landranger 42**

**Three peaks reached by way of good
high paths and one long climb to reach
a wide plateau. A mountain bike will
speed access to the start.**

   Start at a layby on the A86 at the narrows
of Loch Laggan where a bridge leads south
to Luiblea (GR433831). Walk or cycle across
the bridge, and turn left to leave the
collection of houses and climb a stile. The
track accompanies the river before rising
eastwards to a junction. Take the right fork
here and climb to reach another
intersection by a small lochan. Turn left to
continue more easily to the shores of
Lochan na-h-Earba. Leave bikes at the loch:
walk times start from this point. Walk along
the sandy track to the southernmost corner
of the loch where the track forks. Take the
right fork which leads to a path after 300m.
Turn south alongside the Allt Coire Pitridh

and climb a short way until level with a shieling. Turn off the path and ford the burn. Walk up through heather and grasses towards the large bowl of Coire Mór a'Chlachair. At the lip of the corrie, gain the prominent north ridge of Beinn a'Chlachair. Climb steeply along this rocky ridge to reach the summit (GR471781) (2h40). Follow the plateau around the northern corrie and then ENE for 1.5km, and descend northeast over awkward ground to avoid the cliffs overlooking Loch a'Bhealaich Leamhain. This leads down to the main bealach between Geal Charn and Beinn a'Chlachair (GR490800). [Escape: follow the Allt Coire Pitridh westwards back to the start.] Pick up a path rising northwards which climbs to another bealach. Then bear east to climb gentle slopes to the summit of Geal Charn and its magnificent cairn, hidden well back on the plateau (GR504812) (4h40). Return to the last bealach before tackling the short but steep stretch to the summit of Creag Pitridh (GR487815). Bear southwest down grassy slopes to meet the main path along the river. Follow this back to Lochan na h-Earba (6h). Return to the start.

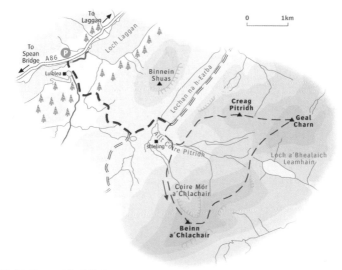

◀ The flats of Laggan and Binnein Shuas

73

Meagaidh's mighty cliffs

Creag Meagaidh Ⓜ(1128m),
Stob Poite Coire Ardair Ⓜ(1054m),
Carn Liath Ⓜ(1006m)

Walk time **8h20** Height gain **1100m**
Distance **21km** OS Map Landranger **34**

**A strenuous, high-level route over
multiple tops with plenty of ascent and
some tricky navigation over the main
peak in mist or snow.**

Start on the A86 at the entrance to the
Creag Meagaidh National Nature Reserve
(GR483873). Walk northwest along the track
to Aberarder, keeping right of the buildings.
An excellent path, reinforced with boards
(slippery in icy conditions), wanders through
scrub and young birch into Coire Ardair.
After a gentle westerly traverse, the high,
vegetated cliffs of Creag Meagaidh come
into view: though spectacular, these broken
cliffs are neglected in summer but become a

mountaineers' playground under winter ice.
The path reaches Lochan a'Choire after
5km. Ford the outlet burn from the loch and
climb southeast over tussocky grass,
following a small burn to reach a tiny
lochan below Sròn a'Ghoire. From the
lochan climb east, avoiding runnels of
awkward scree, to reach a small cairn at the
top. Bear southwest around the corrie,
passing buttresses shaped like flattened
sharks' fins, then climb west to reach Puist
Coire Ardair. Descend gently west over
uniform grass slopes before an easy climb
to the top of Creag Meagaidh: the summit
cairn is west of a narrowing on the plateau
(GR418875) (4h20). Return east for 1km
before descending northwards to join a path
that zigzags alongside fenceposts to The
Window, a sheltered bowl and bealach
above Coire Ardair. [Escape: descend steeply
east over scree to reach Lochan a'Choire

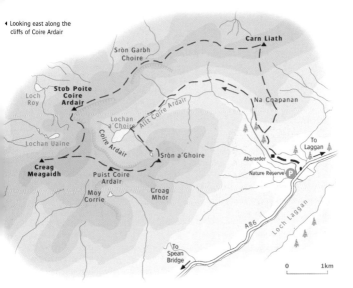

◀ Looking east along the cliffs of Coire Ardair

and the path from Aberarder.] Climb northeast to the summit of Stob Poite Coire Ardair to meet metal fenceposts that lead all the way along the ridge: this gives a fine situation without exposure. Beyond Sròn Garbh Choire the ridge becomes spikier, then drops slightly northwards to a rocky bealach and the remains of a wall. The final ascent to the summit cairn of Carn Liath is straightforward (GR472903) (7h). Return southwest for about 300m to allow a fairly easy descent SSE towards Na Cnapanan. Further down, a path can be joined on the west side of the ridge. Where it later splits, take the right fork to follow posts through occasional boggy sections and birch to the original path. Follow this back to the start (8h20).

Nuts and crampons

With the availability of new materials, climbing became a more popular pursuit in the post-war years. Nuts made from brass or aluminium arrived on the scene, as did the front-pointed crampon: these allowed harder and steeper routes to be attempted. The ascent of Everest in 1953 added to the appeal of the sport. The heroes of the day included Dr Tom Patey, James Marshall and Dougal Haston. Creag Meagaidh, was 'discovered' at this time, and became the scene for many new winter climbs.

Marching to the Piper's tune

Geal Charn (926m)

Walk time 3h20
Approach and return 1h bike or 2h walk
Height gain 700m
Distance 9km + 8km approach and return
OS Map Landranger 35

A lonely mountain reached by way of waterfalls, a secluded lochan and grassy gullies, a surprising contrast to the heather and bog of the Monadh Liath beyond. Use of a mountain bike is possible on the approach.

Start by a bridge over the River Spey on the minor road which serves Garva, 3km west of Laggan (GR584936). (Park about

400m west at the top of the hill.) Pass through a gate on the north side of the bridge, and cycle or walk westwards along a track. This turns north before the dam and soon becomes sandy underfoot: follow it as it climbs past forestry on the right and continues above the Markie Burn to a fence after 4km. Leave bikes here: walk times start from this point. Continue alongside the river until you reach a double set of waterfalls on the west side of the glen. Ford the river at this point. [Variant: if the river is in spate, use the bridge about 500m to the north, then return to the waterfalls.] Climb alongside the falls, following the Piper's Burn (the more westerly of two tributaries) and then keep to fenceposts through boggy terrain to reach the tranquil Lochan a'Choire. Skirt around the south side of the lochan, where the grass slopes drop steeply to the water, to reach a grassy gully between Geal Charn and Beinn Sgiath. It is a steep but enjoyable climb to the bealach above. From here, follow the highest ground to the summit of Geal Charn (GR562988) (2h). Descend gently northeast to some boggy areas, and then contour southeast to join the ridge of Bruach nam Biodag: this ends abruptly. Drop steeply through heather into the glen, keeping to the north side of a fence to join a path. Pass through a gate and watch for the bridge, hidden in the ravine. Across the bridge, the path continues a short way east of the river (this may be difficult to locate) before eventually joining the original track (3h20). Return to the start.

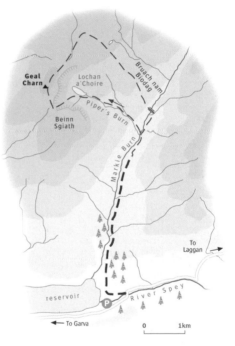

Instruments of war

The bagpipe is the only musical instrument to have also been classed as an instrument of war. In the noise and fury of battle, the *piob-mhór* (great pipe) could be heard at great distances and played a central part in any Highland army. As a result they were outlawed, along with the kilt, following the failed Jacobite uprising of 1745. They flourished again, however, in the large standing armies which won Britain's empire and are still very much part of Highland culture and consciousness.

◄ Laggan village store

Dalwhinnie, Newtonmore and Kingussie sit along the main route between Perth and Inverness. Dalwhinnie means 'meeting place' in Gaelic, and was once a stopover for cattle drovers on the way to southern markets. Newtonmore translates as 'big new town', and grew as crofters who had been cleared from estates settled in the area. General Wade built an ambitious road over the heights of the Corrieyairack Pass to link Fort Augustus on Loch Ness with the Ruthven Barracks at Kingussie. The defeated Bonnie Prince Charlie burnt the barracks on his retreat from Culloden, leaving the landmark ruins.

The Perth-Inverness railway serves the start of seven circuits in this section. Dalwhinnie is the start point for four routes. Two of these are shorter walks: one cuts through the hidden gorge of Dirc Mhór and a second begins with a long trek along Loch Ericht. The other two circuits from Dalwhinnie are long and remote, venturing into the Ben Alder massif. These are best

accessed by mountain bike and can be completed more easily in a two-day trip. Another walk traverses the rounded Drumochter Hills to the south of Dalwhinnie. Two routes start close to the town of Newtonmore to climb the hills above Glen Banchor. A final route begins in the centre of Kingussie.

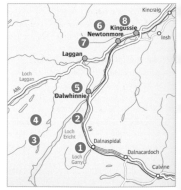

Dalwhinnie to Kingussie

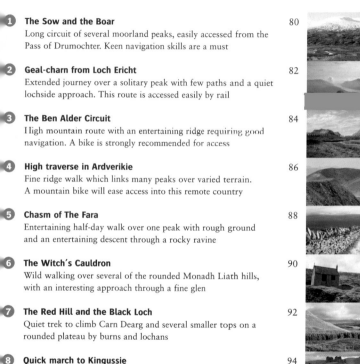

The Sow and the Boar

Sgairneach Mhór Ⓜ(991m),
Beinn Udlamain Ⓜ(1011m),
A´Mharconaich Ⓜ(975m)

Walk time 6h40 Height gain 1000m
Distance 21km OS Map Landranger 42

**A round of several tops, with views of
Loch Ericht and Ben Alder. The route
follows paths and tracks with some
sections of bog. Good navigation is
essential, as there are few features to
guide in poor weather.**

Start at the turn-off for Dalnaspidal Lodge
at the north end of the long stretch of dual
carriageway over the Pass of Drumochter

(GR645733). (Parking on the track between
the road and the railway.) Walk along the
road towards the lodge, cross the railway
and continue along the track for Loch Garry.
Cross two bridges and keep to the loch for
about 1km. Leave the track at a convenient
point and bear due west up gentle, boggy
slopes. After a first false top, the terrain
steepens before reaching Ceann Gorm.
Continue west to the top of Meallan Buidhe
and then northwest along the ridge and
over undulating ground until confronted by
the broad southeast flank of Sgairneach
Mhór. Climb this to gain the wide plateau,
and bear northeast to the summit and trig

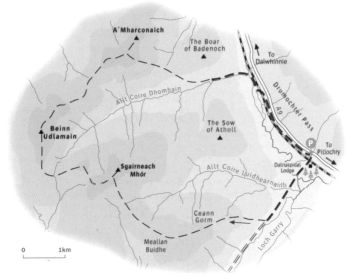

point (GR599731) (3h). The twisting descent gives fine views of Ben Alder: return southwest for 500m and then follow a rounded ridge northeast before dropping westwards to a level area of boggy ground. Ascend the south ridge of Beinn Udlamain and follow fenceposts to the summit. Continue northeast by the posts to a bealach before making the easy ascent to the top of A'Mharconaich: the highest point is located at the northeast end of the summit plateau (GR604763) (5h). There is steep ground around this point so return southwest, keeping the high ground until you find a line of fenceposts. Follow these down to gentler ground to gain a track by the Allt Coire Dhomhain. The track leads east and then veers south to run alongside the railway and the road. Take the tunnel under the railway, and continue south along the track between the road and the railway to Dalnaspidal (6h40).

Drumochter Pass

Flanked by two hogs' backs, the Boar of Badenoch and the Sow of Atholl, this bleak pass was the meeting place of General Wade's military road-builders working north from Dunkeld and south from Inverness. A stone erected in 1729 marks the point at which the no doubt relieved troops met.

◄ Meallan Buidhe and Sgairneach Mhór from Dalnaspidal

Geal-charn from Loch Ericht

Geal-charn ⓜ (917m)

Walk time **7h** Height gain **700m**
Distance **19km** OS Map **Landranger 42**

Long circuit from the highest village in the Highlands with a strenuous approach along the banks of Loch Ericht to climb one of the rounded Drumochter hills.

Start by the petrol station at the south end of Dalwhinnie (GR636842). Take the minor road on the south side of the petrol station, passing a few houses to reach a railway underpass. Go through the underpass to reach a gate for a private track: continue straight on beyond the gate and bear westwards, keeping Loch Ericht to your right. After about 1km, just beyond a cottage, the track ends at a boathouse. Keep to the shore beyond the buildings, following various stalking or animal tracks through the heather, and cross two deer fences by gates. After the second gate, beneath the broken crags with a prominent scar, the terrain underfoot becomes trickier with boulders and scree. These difficulties are short-lived and the impressive Creag Dhubh, sometimes boasting a high waterfall, comes into view. Beyond the last cliffs, at a point level with Ben Alder Lodge on the far side of the loch and where another fence marks a plantation, leave the shore (GR580783) (2h20). Ascend the undulating slopes southeast to the bealach of Coire Fhàr. Turn north and climb the rounded south ridge of Geal-charn to the summit (GR596783) (4h40). Continue northwards to reach a small lochan at Coire Beul an Sporain, from which a track can be joined heading northeast. Follow this for just a short time, as it soon drops to the east. Instead, continue along the high ground to the top of Creagan Mór (GR616805). Drop down to another lochan, and descend northeast into a vast mire of bog and towards the apex of a large plantation. Follow a track along the southeastern boundary of the forest to reach the railway line.

Cross two bridges to gain the intersection between the A9 and the A889 to Dalwhinnie. This leaves a short walk along the minor road back to the village (7h).

◄ Loch Ericht and Geal-charn from Beinn Bheoil

The Ben Alder Circuit

Ben Alder Ⓜ(1148m),
Beinn Bheoil Ⓜ(1019m)

Walk time 6h20 Height gain 900m
Approach and return 4h bike or 7h walk
Distance 15km + 30km approach and
return OS Map Landranger 42

**A great horseshoe route around steep
rocky corries and a high mountain loch,
with easy scrambling in ascent. Use of a
mountain bike is advised for the long
access through remote terrain. Sharp
navigation skills are essential.**

Start from Dalwhinnie Station
(GR634849). Turn right (south) out of the
station to reach a level crossing after 300m.
Cross the railway line and take the gravel
track along the west bank of Loch Ericht.
After 8km, at Ben Alder Lodge, the track
starts to climb through trees and then leads
west over open ground and down to Loch
Pattack. Follow the sandy shore to the
south end and a junction just beyond. Take
the left fork (south) to reach Culra Bothy,
just north of Culra Lodge (GR522762). Leave
bikes here: walk times begin at this point.
Walk 150m south of the bothy: a good path
follows the Allt a'Chaoil-réidhe upstream on
its west bank. Follow the burn for about
2km, past the confluence of the Allt
a'Bhealaich Bheithe and the Allt
a'Bhealaich Dhuibh. Ford the latter at a
convenient point and start to climb south
over or around awkward hummocks towards

◀ Ben Alder and Sgòr Iutharn

the knobbly ridge known as the Long Lethchois, the western boundary of Coire na Lethchois. A narrow path twists its way along the crest of the ridge, sporting short sections of easy scrambling with little exposure. This leads to a cairn on the high plateau of Ben Alder. Climb southwards over gentle scree-laden slopes to grassy terrain, where the Loch a'Bhealaich Bheithe comes into view, to reach the final rocky summit and trig point of Ben Alder (GR496718) (3h). Follow the undulating ground SSW around the rim of the Garbh Choire before bearing southeast to drop to a boulder-strewn niche. Continue to the top of Sròn Bealach Beithe. The main ridge of the peak lures you eastwards, but this leads to steep cliffs: instead, descend southeast over awkward terrain to reach the Bealach Breabag. Climb northeast to the top of Sròn Coire na h-Iolaire and descend the north ridge to another bealach. Climb NNE, keeping west of a rocky outcrop, to reach the flat summit of Beinn Bheoil (GR517717) (5h). Descend by the prominent north ridge and climb a smaller knoll beyond. Continue north until the terrain flattens after 500m, then head northwest off the ridge. After

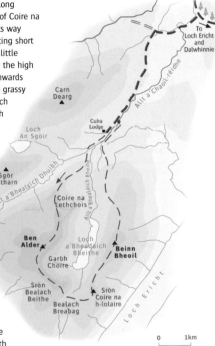

1km of fairly easy terrain, you will come to a renovated path that zigzags down to meet the Allt a'Chaoil-réidhe. A bridge takes you back to the original track just north of the bothy (6h20). Cycle or walk back to the start.

High traverse in Ardverikie

Carn Dearg ⓜ (1034m), **Geal-charn** ⓜ (1132m), **Aonach Beag** ⓜ (1116m), **Beinn Eibhinn** ⓜ (1102m)

Walk time **7h** Height gain **1000m**
Approach and return **3h20 bike or 6h walk**
Distance **20km + 24km** approach and return OS Map **Landranger 42**

Remote peaks and varied terrain make for an interesting circuit. This route follows a long ridge over deep corries and returns by a quiet glen. A mountain bike is recommended for the approach.

Start at Dalwhinnie Station (GR634849). Turn right (south) out of the station to reach a level crossing after 300m. Cross the railway line and take the gravel track along the west bank of Loch Ericht. After 8km, at Ben Alder Lodge, the track starts to climb through trees and then leads west over open ground and down to Loch Pattack. Follow the sandy shore to the south end and a junction just beyond. Leave bikes here: walk times begin at this point. Take the right fork, and follow this track until you reach the first of several dips after about 500m. Leave the track here and bear southwest over heather slopes, passing several cairns. Higher up, the terrain steepens and leads to a broad flat ridge that rises easily WSW to attain a prominent grass spur: this takes you to the summit of

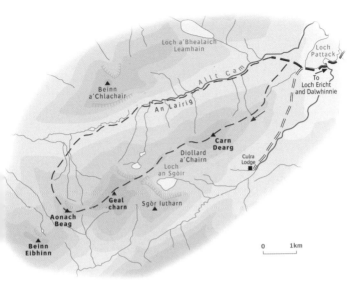

Carn Dearg (GR503764) (2h). Descend west over rockier ground for fine views of Loch an Sgòir and the dark ridge of Sgòr Iutharn to the south. Continue along the fine ridge of Diollard a'Chairn to reach a notch between two corries, a pair of parallel gullies carved in the hillside above. The ridge ahead is steep but holds no surprises, and easy ground is soon reached. Cross the vast plateau of Geal-charn, a great place for a game of shinty, to reach the summit. Descend southwest from the cairn (watching out for the steep western corrie) to a bealach, before tackling the final ridge to the summit of Aonach Beag (GR458742) (4h20). Descend the rocky north ridge without difficulty until the slopes level out.

[Variant: to climb Beinn Eibhinn, descend the southwest ridge of Aonach Beag to a bealach, then climb west around the corrie to the summit. Descend the north ridge, keeping west to avoid scree, before descending into the corrie. Traverse northeast over boggy terrain to join the north ridge of Aonach Beag.] Descend northeast across the lower slopes of Coire na Coichille to reach An Lairig, a remote glen. There is a path, little used but in good repair with even a few small bridges. This keeps to the south side of the glen over a quaggy bealach and along the Allt Cam. After about 6km, it begins to rise eastwards, gaining width to become the original track to Loch Pattack (7h). Return to the start.

◄ Peaks of Ardverikie: Aonach Beag from Geal-charn

Chasm of The Fara

The Fara ⓒ (911m)

Walk time **4h40** Height gain **500m**
Distance **13km** OS Map **Landranger 42**

Fairly short but exciting route over one peak with a mix of good access tracks and rough walking. Some sections of this walk can be boggy after rain.

Start 1.5km north of Dalwhinnie at a gravel track marked as a right of way, which leads to the house of Allt-an-t-Sluic (GR636863). (Park 800m towards Dalwhinnie at the Military Road junction.) Follow the track west for about 700m, pass through a gate and continue beyond. About midway between the gate and the house, a grassy track branches left. Take this to ford the burn, and then follow it WSW up through heather. After about 1.5km, where the track disappears, continue more awkwardly over the gradually receding heather to reach the prominent northeast ridge of The Fara. Follow this southwards, passing clusters of small boulders, to reach

the summit with its incongruous giant cairn, well-fashioned wall and occasional outcrops (GR598844) (2h20). From the summit, follow old fenceposts northwest as they descend the main ridge of Meall Liath and then trend off the west side of the spur. Lower down, where the ground steepens, bear westwards (left) to leave the line of posts and avoid high crags. This gives a way down to the rocky chasm of Dirc Mhór, which can be easily entered from the south side. Drop down through the ravine, negotiating the boulders which have calved off the sides and wedged together to form a mosaic of micro-granite. Further down beyond The Sentinel, a steep, compact crag on the right, the terrain underfoot becomes easier, descending through trees by fencing. This leads down to a wide glen with a web of powerlines. Follow the glen eastwards over grass and heather. After 1.5km, you will come to a track which fords the burn of Allt-an-t-Sluic several times to reach the house: this should be circumnavigated on the south side. Follow the original track back to the road (4h40).

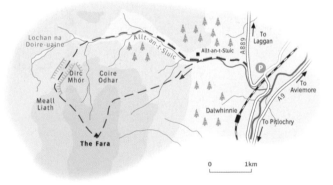

Dalwhinnie Distillery

At 358m (1173ft) above sea level, Dalwhinnie is the highest whisky distillery in Scotland, built here to gain the best access to the pure waters of Lochan na Doire-uaine. Not surprisingly, it can get very windy and cold but, whatever the weather, it is the duty of the distillery manager to take daily readings of temperature, pressure and rainfall as the distillery is also an official recording station of the Meteorological Office.

◀ On the summit of The Fara

The Witch's Cauldron

A'Chailleach ⓜ (930m),
Carn Sgùlain ⓜ (920m)

Walk time 6h Height gain 800m
Distance 16km OS Map Landranger 35

Several rounded hills with few mountain paths and even fewer features, making good navigation skills useful. This walk is easily accessed from Newtonmore with a good approach on tracks through a picturesque glen.

Start at the end of the public road in Glen Banchor, a short walk from Newtonmore (GR692997). Find a path on the west side of a mound by the car park. This leads north to a track that passes a plantation and then continues on the east bank of the Allt a'Chaorainn. Where the track halts, double back 40m to find a rickety wooden bridge in the trees. Cross the bridge, and follow a vague path along the west bank for 300m to reach an old fence. Leave the path to follow a burn northwest. This leads to a shelter and an old path after 800m. Continue to climb northwest: the path steepens before levelling out into boggy terrain. Watch for a path which leads due north and then climbs directly to the summit of A'Chailleach (the Witch) (GR681042) (2h40). Descend northwest on springy grass to a steep-sided trench, and then climb northeast across bog to the summit of Carn Sgùlain with its rusted fenceposts (GR683058) (3h40). Descend directly east and then southeast across undulating terrain to Am Bodach before joining wooden fenceposts to climb a hump, on whose top the few boulders look quite out of place. Descend WSW along the vague ridge over Beinn Bhuidhe and, when you tire of bog, drop down to a path on the east bank of the Allt a'Chaorainn. This path improves

Ossian

James MacPherson grew up near Kingussie and his infamy lies in the release of the works of Ossian in 1765. This Homeric opus of prose and poetry concerned the heroic exploits of Fingal and his son Ossian, mythical warriors who roamed Scotland during Dalriadic times, and whose legacy is shared in Ireland. MacPherson claimed the stories were original and that he had just discovered them, but the truth emerged later: he had written them himself. To his credit, MacPherson travelled extensively from 1760 to record as much second-hand material as possible, interviewing local storytellers and historians. Regardless of the art involved, though, he is remembered as a fraud and not as a poet.

further down and leads to the original track just a short distance from the start (6h).

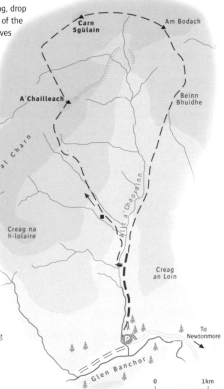

◄ Shelter above the Allt a'Chaorainn

91

The Red Hill and the Black Loch

Carn Dearg ⓜ (945m)

Walk time **6h40** Height gain **600m**
Distance **20km** OS Map **Landranger 35**

A journey that starts with a river crossing and follows a mountain burn to reach a high corrie lochan. Height is gained gradually to climb a single peak and continue across an undulating plateau. Navigation skills would be useful on the rolling moorland.

Start at the end of the public road in Glen Banchor, a short walk from Newtonmore (GR692997). Walk west along the track,

cross the bridge and continue through two gates. After 1km the track leads to Glenballoch Farm: immediately opposite the house there is a gate on the left. Pass through the gate, and follow the signs and the path ahead as it swings through another gate to accompany the river. Where the Allt Ballach joins the River Calder, keep below the ruins and wade across the burn. Beyond the steep river embankments, start to shadow the north bank of the Allt an Lochain Duibh upstream. After 2km, where the terrain is dominated by moraines, the path rises above the east side of the burn

before climbing more steeply by a cascade to reach the dark Loch Dubh in Coire nan Laogh, where there is a rough shelter. Climb heathery slopes due east to the ridgeline, then follow it north to reach first a subsidiary top and then the summit of Carn Dearg (the Red Cairn) with its steep east-facing crags (GR635024) (4h). Descend northwest before making the gentle ascent of the flat-topped Carn Bàn. Now follow

fenceposts northeast, dipping and rising over bog and rock. Aim for the rounded top of Carn Ballach, and then drop southwards to the top of Meall na Ceardaidh. Descend steep grass slopes from this peak, keeping southeast to aim for the Allt Fionndrigh. Cross the burn to find a path on the other side: this soon becomes a track and leads easily back to the farm. It is a short walk to the start (6h40).

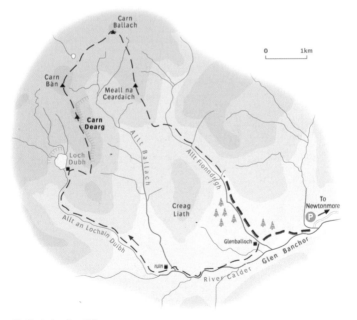

◄ Glen Banchor from Creag Liath

93

Quick march to Kingussie

Creag Mhór (660m), **Creag Dubh** (787m)

Walk time 4h + detour 1h
Height gain 500m
Distance 10km OS Map Landranger 35

One peak above a fine loch with good access tracks from the town centre. Rough terrain higher up and some intricate route-finding on return.

Start at the traffic lights at the centre of Kingussie (GR757007). Walk steeply up Ardbroilach Road above the east bank of the Allt Mór. After about 1km, the road levels out and enters the Pitmain Lodge estate. Continue northwards past the golf course and through light forest to reach a green and white Nissen hut just after crossing the river. From the west side of the hut, take the track that leads north through old pine. Leave the forest and continue on the track until it curves around some moraines after 300m. At this point, leave the track and head westwards over rough heather to gain the craggy west ridge of Creag Mhór. Deep undergrowth and boulders make this hard going, but the ridge gives good views of Loch Gynack. After reaching the top of the first knoll and cairn, descend into a dip and climb a second hill. It's an easy descent through the broken cliffs on the north side to reach the flatter third knoll, which marks the top of Creag Mhór (GR735029) (2h). Drop northwest to a bealach. [Detour: climb northwest over

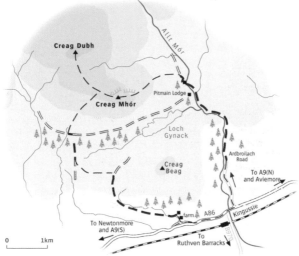

humps and bumps to reach the summit of Creag Dubh. Return the same way (add 1h).] Descend southwest over rough ground towards the large plantation, following a small burn lower down to reach a track and gate. Pass through the gate and take a second track through the forest break, emerging after 400m by another gate with two tracks just beyond: take the lesser track ESE across the open moor. Where this very soon starts to fade, head east towards some old walls and a fence. Cross this by a

gate and pick up another grassy track that skirts around a ridge above the fine glen beneath Creag Beag. Go through a gate to shortly reach the end of the track below some houses. Pass through a gate on the right and drop down through a field to emerge behind the farm buildings of Pitmain Farm. Walk east on the farm track to the main road. Follow the cycle path and pavement (or the tracks and roads of Middle Terrace) back into the centre of Kingussie (4h).

Ruthven Barracks

Built as a Hanoverian garrison following the 1715 Jacobite Rising, the Ruthven Barracks were designed to hold a full complement of 120 men. In 1745, however, a Jacobite attack was repelled by only a dozen men – although they fled a year later when the insurgents returned with canon. Following Culloden, battle-weary Jacobites rallied here to await orders but were told to seek shelter as best they could by their defeated Prince.

◀ The Ruthven Barracks at Kingussie

Index

Ⓜ **Munros** are mountains in Scotland above 914m (3000ft). (Named after Sir Hugh Munro who compiled the first list in 1891.)

Ⓒ **Corbetts** are peaks between 762m and 914m (2500ft and 3000ft) which have a drop of at least 152m (500ft) on all sides. (Named after John Corbett who drew up the list and made the first ascent.)